The **3rd Edition**

LEADER'S COMPASS

A Personal Leadership Philosophy
Is Your Foundation for Success

ED RUGGERO and DENNIS F. HALEY

ISBN: 978-0-972-73238-3

Library of Congress Control Number: 2013956702

Academy Leadership books are available at special quantity discounts to use as premiums and sales promotions, or for use in corporate training programs. For more information, please call Academy Leadership at 866-783-0630, or write to: 10120 Valley Forge Circle, King of Prussia, PA 19406.

www.academyleadership.com

Printed in the United States of America

It is a rare organization that does not have some sort of mission statement, organizational philosophy or values proposition to guide members and focus their work. Most leaders recognize that developing these clearly articulated statements is time well spent; they help keep the organization on track and pointed toward clear goals. A written leadership philosophy, which we call *The Leader's Compass*, achieves the same thing on a personal level; it lets people know what you expect, what you value, how you'll act, and how you'll measure performance, with the additional benefits of making the workplace less stressful and more productive. And, like a compass, it helps to keep you, the leader, on course.

"Often leaders have the best intentions, but people cannot read their minds. That's why it's important to declare yourself: Tell people why you choose to lead and the code you live by."
Douglas Conant
Former President & CEO, Campbell Soup Company

Table of Contents

The Command Leadership Philosophy

In the 1980s, the United States Navy did a study to determine why some ships performed well consistently in every measure of effectiveness, from inspections to combat drills, whereas others were consistent in average performance. The answer was deceptively simple: it all started with the skipper. The results did not surprise experienced Navy men and women; a sailor can tell a lot about the command climate on a ship simply by going aboard, looking around at maintenance, cleanliness and seaworthiness, and talking to the crew to determine their spirit and attitude. The pivotal role played by the commander is underscored by this dictum, which is gospel throughout all the nation's armed forces: *The commander is responsible for everything the unit does or fails to do.*

Talk about your straightforward guidelines.

Leadership plays the central role in what military units can accomplish. The same is true in business. This is why a good boss—a good leader—is responsible and is out in front of the organization.

Because leadership begins with the boss—with the commander, in military terms—both the U.S. Army and the U.S. Navy require new commanders to write a leadership philosophy, a written document that lets subordinates know: this is where I stand, and this is what I want. This explicit statement of standards and expectations provides general guidance on what to do and how to do it. In addition, if the boss's actions are consistent with his or her stated beliefs, subordinates learn to trust the leader. A boss who says one thing and does another, or states one set of values and lives by another, may get people to follow during easy times, but when things get tough, either because of economic or business uncertainty, because of pressures in the marketplace, or just tough competition, people want leaders of character.

What follows is a fictional account of how one leader developed his *Leader's Compass.*

Acknowledgments

Many people made possible the publication of this book, especially the affiliates of Academy Leadership who developed and presented *The Leader's Compass* in numerous seminars. Their experience in coaching thousands of clients in writing personal leadership philosophies gave us the material from which to build this resource for all aspiring leaders.

Thanks to Captain H.J. Halliday, United States Navy (Retired), former skipper of the USS *Nevada*, whose command leadership philosophy is the basis for the one in this book.

Thanks to Suzanne Pellican of Intuit, whose leadership philosophy is the basis for the version belonging to the fictional Linda Hutchinson. Suzanne wrote her first draft after attending the Gettysburg Leadership Experience, then worked hard to make it even better for her team.

Thanks to the many men and women of the U.S. Navy and the U.S. Army who, over the years, have taken the time to teach the authors about leadership. Thanks also to the many commanders, professors, cadets, midshipmen, spouses and children who have been a part of our individual learning experiences.

CHAPTER 1

Guy Cedrick is a big man with wide shoulders, only the intimation of a neck, and hands the size of dinner plates. Even hunched over his drawing table, with design samples and color palettes around him, he looks like a linebacker who has wandered in from football practice. He enjoys surprising people by telling them he's an artist.

Guy did major in art history, as well as marketing, at Notre Dame, where he carried a respectable workload and GPA in spite of all the time he spent under the watchful eyes of the Irish coaching staff. Wandering to Philadelphia after graduation, he toyed with the idea of walking on at the Eagles training camp. Over that first summer he took a part-time job at a marketing firm in a section of low-slung, red brick homes and offices called Old City, and soon found that he loved the work. The hours he spent each day at a drafting table or in front of his computer appealed to his sense of order, his need to get his hands on the work. The design meetings he attended, with the clients and the rest of the creative team, appealed to the artist in him. The meetings were unstructured and inspired, with lots of talk about the buyer's experience, ink colors and lighting of photographs.

Guy started as a print designer at The Eaton Group and over time was trusted to develop entire marketing campaigns for clients. He had autonomy, creative license and a comfortable budget, and despite a few weeks of feeling like a fugitive, when it became clear that football season was going to start without him, he let go of his NFL fantasies.

When the creative and marketing team grew to five people, Old Man Eaton took to referring to Guy as the "team leader" for the operation. In reality, that just meant Guy took notes at meetings and left copies on his colleagues' drawing tables. He had been with the company six years, had married, become a father, and had just passed his twenty-ninth birthday when Old Man Eaton retired and J. Walter Eaton, number-one son and business school grad, took over. The new boss enjoyed the social aspects of the work: the client lunches and afternoons on the golf course. He introduced himself as "J.W.," but nearly everyone at the company referred to him, out of earshot, as "Wally." Where the old man had worn a suit or a blazer and tie every day, Wally liked Italian jackets in busy patterns, with white silk shirts that showed off the perpetual island-vacation look he maintained with the help of a tanning bed in his home gym.

J.W. came on board with the idea that growth was just the thing for The Eaton Group. One day he walked up to Guy's desk beside the elevator on the big, loft-like second floor and announced that he was going to double the size of the marketing group by purchasing an interactive media company.

"We're going to bring in seven more people, with a whole suite of video-editing equipment, plus more graphics and animation stuff," J.W. announced grandly, waving his arm at the already crowded area behind Guy's desk.

"Great," Guy said, wondering why he hadn't been brought in on the decision earlier. He also wondered if Wally had a plan for integrating the traditional marketing function and the newer capabilities of the interactive media folks.

"What are we going to do to keep them busy?" Guy asked.

"Grow, baby, grow," J.W. said, winking at Guy, as if that explained it all.

That was in September. Before Halloween rolled around, there were, indeed, seven more people—programmers, video editors, animators, graphic artists and project managers— crammed into what had been a tight space for the original eight. The seven—four women and three men—had been part of an advertising company, Kensington, that went belly up when its owner flew out of the country with $1.1 million in company cash and a former hand model and Dallas Cowboys cheerleader twenty years his junior. Rumor had them on the beach in some island country that had no extradition treaty with the United States, where they'd left a mountain of debt and a group of employees who felt betrayed. J.W. got the company at fire-sale prices, and although the folks who joined Guy on the second floor were happy to have jobs, they were not exactly lighthearted about all the changes.

Guy met one of the new people, Linda Hutchinson, when she marched up to his desk on the morning of her arrival, her coat still on, and announced, "There's no ladies room on this floor."

"Uhh," Guy replied, standing behind his desk. Linda was only a few inches shorter than Guy, which made her at least six-foot-one. She had short dark hair, clear skin and tiny eyeglasses that did nothing to diminish a direct, discomfiting stare. She balanced a paper coffee cup in one hand and a large black bag in the other; when Guy stuck out his big hand, she made no move to take it.

"I'm Guy," he said, dropping the hand to his side after a few long seconds.

"Congratulations," she said. "Now where's the ladies room?"

"That restroom over there is sort of coed," he answered, gesturing to the far corner of the floor. He used to be able to see the corner, where a refrigerator, coffee stand and mail bins formed an artificial wall that shielded the restroom door from the rest of the open room. Now the view was blocked by several piles of equipment that had been delivered and not put away. Thick black cables, looped and taped like lariats, lay on top of the metal cabinets and computer boxes the movers had delivered over the weekend. Guy wondered why no one was unpacking and installing the new equipment.

Linda tapped a long fingernail on Guy's desk and cocked her head to one side a little bit.

"Guy, how many people work on this floor now?"

"Fifteen," he said, feeling a bit as if he'd been called in front of the class, where he was about to reveal his ignorance.

"That's what I count, too," Linda said. "And that's too many people to share one bathroom. Especially because you boys are so … sloppy."

"Uh-huh," was all Guy could think of to say.

"I'd suggest you get another bathroom put in up here," Linda continued. She spoke slowly, as if Guy might not understand the concept of separate facilities.

Linda dropped her bag, put her coffee cup down on Guy's desk, bent over and, taking a marker from his cup of pens and a sheet of company stationery from his desktop, she wrote "LADIES ROOM" in thick black letters. She pulled a piece of tape from the dispenser on his bookshelf, retrieved her things and, without saying anything else to Guy, threaded her way across the floor toward the bathroom. Guy couldn't see the door from where he stood, but he assumed the sign, and the new restriction, had gone into effect immediately.

Guy dropped into his chair.

"Oh boy," he said to himself. He fished a legal pad from the pile on his desk and made his way to the top of the stairs. No one, he noticed, was doing anything to get the equipment sorted out. Computer parts sat on sound consoles, which were pushed up against video screens and racks full of digital tapes. Not only was the newly delivered stuff sitting in precarious-looking piles on the floor, but also the old equipment was blocked in; not much would get done in here today.

"Peter," Guy called to one of his graphic designers. Peter was thirty, although Guy was convinced he thought of himself as a twenty-three-year-old. He had a ponytail and a penchant for double lattes, which he drank while reading the newspaper. Guy thought he should read the paper and drink his coffee before he got to work.

Peter looked up from the sports page; he was sitting beside his console, unable to pull his chair closer because of a pile of black metal boxes the movers had installed where the chair belonged.

"I'd like to get that initial design today," Guy called. Peter was supposed to finish a demo CD for a client, one that showed some of the Group's recent work.

Peter gestured at the equipment blocking access to his workstation, then shrugged. "What do I do with this stuff?"

"Who does it belong to?" Guy asked.

Peter pointed with his thumb at four people standing near the refrigerator. Linda had traded her coffee cup for a big plastic water bottle.

"Can you figure out some way to get it set up so that we can get some work done here?" Guy asked.

"They don't want anyone touching their equipment until the tech people come to hook it all up."

Guy felt a slight flutter below his rib cage. He hadn't arranged for the company that serviced the computer graphics and editing equipment to send someone out to make sure it was all hooked up properly.

"Pete ... See what you can do, all right?"

Guy noticed the crowd from Kensington watching him. Linda said something he couldn't hear, and everyone around her laughed.

The team leaders called it "Wally Time," which actually referred to two things: their boss's flexible approach to time—he was routinely late to his own meetings—and to the *Alice in Wonderland* quality of time spent in Wally's company.

Guy sat down next to Ellen Grady, who had been promoted to chief financial officer by Old Man Eaton just before Wally took over. Ellen, a fifty-year-old marathon runner, was smart and direct, and didn't suffer fools lightly. Rumor was that Ellen wouldn't have been Wally's first choice for CFO, probably because she wasn't afraid to tell him when he was wrong.

Ellen looked up from a report she was editing to give Guy a quick smile.

"How are you?" she asked. She flipped open her cell phone and punched in a number, then made eye contact with Guy again.

"Good," he said. "I'm good, thanks."

J.W. Eaton breezed in twenty minutes late, talking golf with a man Guy had never seen before.

"You play golf?" Ellen asked Guy, her hand over the mouthpiece of her phone.

Guy shook his head.

"And you're a team leader?" she said, sounding surprised.

Guy had hoped Wally would talk about how the company was going to integrate its two new acquisitions—besides the seven people from Kensington, J.W. had also added six people to Eaton's sales force. Instead, he introduced the visitor.

"This is my good friend John Hulton, who is going to revolutionize the home mortgage industry," J.W. said grandly.

The first thing one noticed about John Hulton was his hair: a rich salt-and-pepper mix, it sat on his head like it was cast from something hard, concrete or brushed steel. It looked bulletproof. J.W. continued to gush.

"Right now the process of applying for a home loan and closing on a home is only slightly less cumbersome than, say, building an interstate highway through some rich neighborhood. There are all sorts of unnecessary steps and inefficiencies, all of which cost the customer a lot of money.

"John Hulton wants to make applying for a loan and closing on a home as easy as buying a car," J.W. said.

"Buying a hamburger," Hulton corrected.

"Or buying a hamburger," J.W. parroted.

"We have an efficient, highly replicable process that delivers customer satisfaction units in a timely manner, with little or no need for looped processes that just waste time and wind up costing the customer money and interfering with our efficiency paradigms," Hulton said.

Guy felt a great temptation to look at Ellen, seated beside him, and say, "What?" But J.W. wore a beatific smile, and was nodding as if Hulton made perfect sense.

"And, of course, because standardization is one of our key market advantages, we'll want to standardize our sales force's approach to customers," Hulton continued. "It's about controlling the customer's experience, and that begins with controlling the sales rep's experience. We offer solutions to our customers, and we'll start by creating solutions for our sales team."

Next to Guy, Ellen had drawn an oversized question mark on her tablet.

"Concord will have a national sales force meeting here in Philadelphia at the end of the year," J.W. said. "And Eaton is going to deliver the marketing strategy, as well as the sales tools the reps will use. At the conference, they'll be introduced to a multimedia sales approach, and they'll leave with the same tool on a CD. The sales presentation will be modular, so they can pick and choose what parts they want to use on any given sales call.

"Guy, I want you to head this up, of course," J.W. said.

Guy noticed John Hulton looking at him, and he recognized the look, which he'd been getting since he reached fifteen and six-foot-three. It said "big dumb jock."

"Sounds like fun," Guy lied.

Hulton stood abruptly, and J.W. practically leaped from his seat.

"I have a plane to catch," Hulton announced.

"Will I be able to meet with you soon?" Guy asked. "Or is there someone in your organization I should deal with?"

"My people will give you a call," Hulton said without smiling.

"Great," Guy answered, but he was thinking, *My people? My people? Who the heck says that? Who are you, Moses?*

After the meeting, Guy waited for J.W. on the first floor.

"A real visionary, that guy," J.W. said as he walked into his office and motioned for Guy to follow.

"Does he always talk like that?" Guy asked. "I've heard some bad cases of marketing-speak before, but he's way ahead of the pack."

J.W. waved his hand dismissively. Guy knew J.W. saw himself as a captain of industry, buying sports franchises and flying in corporate jets, and this business with Concord had filled his head with dollar signs and growth percentages. Hulton's inability to express himself might have set off alarm bells for the people who'd have to work with him, but it wasn't enough to trouble J.W.

"Now you see why I brought in those digital animators and video folks," J.W. said. He sat back and studied his fingernails, which shone uniformly.

"You want me to create a marketing campaign, a multimedia presentation and a sales CD with the folks who just arrived today?"

"Of course," J.W. said happily. "You'll have them integrated in no time, I'm sure. How are things going upstairs?"

"Fine, fine," Guy said. He didn't think J.W. would bother to climb the stairs to the second floor, and so he wouldn't see the piles of equipment stacked around the room.

"For your new unit to be an asset to the company, you've got to get your people on the same sheet of music and moving in the right direction. Keep them motivated," J.W. said.

"Of course," Guy answered, but J.W. was already moving down the hall toward the front entrance and the parking lot outside.

Guy had called a meeting for 11 a.m., but he wasn't sure what he was going to say. He certainly had no idea how to translate J. W.'s vague advice—get your people on the same sheet of music—into anything useful for the fourteen people who would soon be sitting around the table, sipping coffee and watching him.

He called his wife, Melanie.

"How's the new team?" she asked brightly.

"Great," he said, looking around the open floor, with its piles of equipment like some kind of electronics graveyard. Guy's penchant for a messy office was a standing joke between them and the main reason Melanie did not want him to have a home office, but things on the second floor were annoying even him.

"So, I have this meeting," he said. "Staff meeting."

"And?" Melanie asked.

"Not sure what I'm going to say."

"What did you learn in Wally World?"

"That J.W. has his nails done," Guy said. "And he told me to get my team on the same sheet of music, or something like that."

Melanie laughed. "Sounds like a football coach interviewed at halftime. 'Well, we have to move the ball and play hard and put some points on the board, blah, blah, blah.'"

"That's what I was thinking."

Guy heard their four-year-old daughter, Donna, asking Melanie a question. When Melanie said, "Just a minute, sweetie," Donna became more insistent.

"What do you think I should say?" Guy asked.

Melanie switched back and forth between the telephone conversation and the one at home.

"I don't know, honey. ... Donna, I said you could have that when I get off the phone. ... You've got about ninety years of school under your belt. Surely they must have talked about how to supervise people in one of those classes ... Donna *Cedrick* ... or in one of those conferences you're always going to."

Guy had a vague memory of an offering at a recent trade conference, something about managing or leading. Or was it optimizing and strategizing? It didn't matter; he had stayed away.

"I guess," Guy said into the phone. In reality, in all his years of schooling (a dual major undergrad with an MBA earned at night) and on-the-job training, Guy had never had a single hour's worth of formal preparation for his new role as a leader.

"You'll figure it out, honey," Melanie said.

Guy could tell she had the phone pinched between her chin and shoulder. Whatever was going on with Donna took two hands.

"You're in the fast reading group," Melanie said. "How hard could it be?"

By 11:15 a.m., Guy had a better idea how hard this was going to be. There were only seven people in the conference room.

"Where is everyone?" he asked.

Andy Smythe, who was one of the original Eaton Group people and who was biologically incapable of being late for anything, shook his head and made a sound that might have been tsk tsk.

Linda Hutchinson asked, "Is this how meetings work here? Should I plan on coming fifteen minutes late from now on?"

By 11:20 a.m. he had eleven of fourteen, and Guy started talking. A young woman and a middle-aged man with round shoulders and a black beard walked in a couple of minutes later. Guy said nothing to them but kept talking about how excited he was to work with such a group of *professionals*—he emphasized that word and looked at the two latecomers, hoping they'd pick up a vibe. Guy had a yellow legal tablet in front of him on the table, but it was blank. He thought he used J.W.'s cliché about the same sheet of music, and he managed to work in one of his own, something vaguely nautical, about all pulling in the same direction. It sounded clever in his head, but the group just looked bored. Linda Hutchinson rolled her eyes, and Guy just wanted the meeting to end.

"Do you have a tech crew coming in to assemble all this equipment?" Linda asked.

"I'll have to get one in here," Guy said, thinking that the completely truthful answer sounded more like, "Nope, because I forgot." He didn't have to say it for Linda to get the point.

"Do you want us to just go home for the day?" she asked. "I mean, there's not much we can do here, right?"

Before he could answer, Pete with the ponytail and double latte chimed in. "She's right, you know. I can't even get to my console."

"I'll help you move that stuff so you can," Guy answered, happy to have some sort of plan. "I want that CD to go out of here today, because we have a new project to get hold of."

Guy explained the Concord work as best he could with the limited knowledge he had.

"I'll take care of the initial meetings with the folks from Concord," he said, which let everyone else off the hook. He didn't mention the deadline, which was a little more than six weeks away. Instead, he helped Peter push and shove the equipment around the floor to make some room. The younger man groaned like an Olympic power lifter.

"I'd like to be involved in this mortgage company project," Peter told Guy.

"Yeah? I think J.W. is going to have a lot of interest in this one," Guy said. "But I can try to keep him from calling you every ten seconds or so."

"You'll also have to coordinate the work of the multimedia team," Guy said.

"Of course," Peter agreed.

In the past, Guy had personally overseen the bigger-budget projects himself. He gave out assignments to his team, they reported back to him at every step, and he coordinated the whole thing. Now, with a bigger staff, he supposed that he'd have to hand off some of that responsibility. Peter would not have been his first choice, but he figured that maybe if things got busy, Peter would stop reading the paper at his desk every morning.

"OK," Guy told him. "I'll want to sit in on the first meeting with the people from Concord, hear what they've got in mind."

"I'll ask around the team, too," Peter said. "See who else is interested and who has some ideas."

"Make sure you ask Linda," Guy said. He had no idea why the woman had a chip on her shoulder, but he hoped getting her involved in a project right away would help her lighten up.

Back at his desk, Guy found a "To Do" list he'd started. At the top of the list he added, "Write memo about tardiness at meetings." He looked at "tardiness" and decided it sounded like grammar school, but he couldn't think of another word for it. Then, above that, up near the top of the page, he wrote, "Leadership training?"

The tools hung in a neat row, longest to shortest: leaf rake, garden rake, hoe, long-handled shovel, garden spade, and so on, all of them well used but clean. The lawnmower was swept free of grass clippings. It was Saturday morning, and Guy had walked to his neighbor's garage to borrow a tool.

"You like things neat, I see," Guy said by way of a compliment.

"I come by it honestly," Stanley offered. "Twenty-six years in the Navy."

Stanley Sabato and his wife, Margaret, were Guy and Melanie's next-door neighbors; they'd been the first to welcome the young couple to the neighborhood. During the holidays, the Sabatoes brought Italian pastries to Guy and Melanie from their favorite markets in the city, as well as little presents for Donna. Stanley let Guy borrow tools the younger man hadn't acquired yet in his two years as a homeowner.

Guy, who had never been in the military and whose ideas about the service came from war movies, said, "Lots of inspections and things?"

"Yeah, but it's also the best way to operate, if you want to be efficient. On a ship, with limited space, you have to be efficient."

Stanley pulled a pruning hook from the end of the row and examined it. He was not a big man—his head, with a thick shock of white hair, didn't come up to Guy's shoulder—but he exuded a calm energy. He never hurried but looked as if he could keep the same steady, deliberate pace for days on end. Stanley had dark eyes and serious crow's feet, and Guy imagined him squinting out from the bridge of some ship. Stanley had left the mostly Italian neighborhoods of South Philadelphia when he was seventeen, but the years had done little to diminish his accent. He communicated with hands and facial gestures almost as much as with words.

"You have to know what assets you have—gotta be able to see them at a glance—if you're going to use the right tool for the right job."

Guy had no idea why Stanley's comment about tools made him think of his team of editors, animators, and designers—probably because he didn't know their strengths—but he would eventually be grateful that it prompted his next question.

"You ever been in charge? A management role?" Guy asked.

"Sure," Stanley said. "Except the Navy calls it leadership, not management."

"What's the difference?" Guy asked.

"Short answer?" Stanley asked. "Management is about stuff; leadership is about people."

He handed Guy the pruning hook, pointed out how the hinged blade could be fixed at different angles.

"Don't they overlap?" Guy asked. "Leadership and management?"

"Sure. Lots of leaders have to be concerned with physical assets—stuff—in addition to their people. But you can be a manager without being a leader."

"Because you just deal in stuff?"

"Because you just deal in stuff, or because you treat your people like stuff. That's why I never took to this idea of referring to human beings as 'assets,' as if they were printing presses or forklifts."

Margaret came to the garage door.

"Would either of you home improvement heroes like some coffee? I just made a fresh pot."

Guy accepted the coffee and Stanley's invitation to sit in the sunny breakfast nook off the kitchen. From where he sat, Guy could see into his own backyard, where an autumn wind had cracked a thick limb on a pin oak tree. The pruning hook lay on the patio outside; he'd get to the job eventually.

Guy talked for fifteen minutes about the changes at The Eaton Group. Stanley listened, posed a few questions, and nodded sympathetically from time to time. When Guy finished, he thought Stanley would talk about Linda Hutchinson and how Guy had to rein her in, or Guy's mistake in not scheduling the tech crew to set up the editing suite, or about "Wally time." Instead, Stanley asked a simple question.

"What did you say you wanted to do about the people coming late to your meeting?"

"I was going to write a memo to the team," Guy said. When Stanley said nothing, Guy added, "A policy, you know."

Still nothing from Stanley. The old man appeared to be studying something in the bottom of his coffee cup.

"What do you think I should do?"

"Heck, I don't know," Stanley said. "I've never been in the business world. But tell me this. Was anyone on time for the meeting?"

"Sure, a couple of people were there early; then a few more trickled in. Two were, like, twenty minutes late."

"Were you on time?"

"I guess so."

Stanley smiled. "It was a yes-or-no question, hotshot."

"Yes," Guy said. Then, "I might have been a couple of minutes late."

"Well then, to start, you have to be on time for your own meetings. People will take their cues from you, and what you *do* is more important than all the memos you could write in a year."

Guy thought of J.W. keeping everyone waiting while he talked about golf.

"Right," Guy said.

"Next: no memo."

"Why not?"

"Because the people who were on time don't need it; sending it to them will be insulting. It will mean you didn't notice they were on time.

"Second: you were late, so you're not really in a position to talk about other people being late, at least not without admitting your mistake.

"Third: the people who need it most will probably ignore the memo anyway."

"Why would they do that?" Guy asked.

"They'll think you're not really serious about this, because writing a memo is a chicken way of handling it."

"How do I reach them?"

"After you get yourself in gear, you talk to them individually."

Guy knew that many people were intimidated by his size; it was an asset that had worked for him on the football field. Off the field, he almost never had to confront people, which was a good thing, because the truth was that he didn't like confrontation. He especially didn't like squaring off against women; it made him feel like a bully.

"You mean I have to confront them?"

"Did I say 'confront'? That word has a bad reputation. I said, 'talk to them.' Politely. Assume that they want things to run as smoothly as possible, just as you do."

"What about the fact that I forgot to bring the tech crews in to set up the studio?"

"Have you fixed the problem?"

"Yes. Got them in yesterday."

"Well, you screwed up, and everyone knows it. Nothing to do but say, 'I screwed up.'"

"OK," Guy said, picturing Linda smirking at him.

"But you're not the only one who should have thought of this, right? I mean, these people have been around. Someone else might have reminded you to schedule the support guys."

"Right."

"So you've got to let them know that you rely on them to help you anticipate problems like this. And that means, when they come up with an idea, you've got to listen."

"Of course," Guy said, as if it were the most obvious thing in the world.

"When people are upset, it's harder to listen to them," Stanley said.

"Why is that?"

"Well, let's say you work for me and you're upset about what you think is some lame-brain decision I've made. In a situation like that, as soon as you open your mouth, I go into a defensive mode and my wheels are turning, trying to come up with an answer. So instead of listening, I'm concentrating on what I'm going to say, thinking about how your argument doesn't hold water, thinking about what a jerk you are and how wrong you are about me."

"Oh," Guy said, recognizing a bit of himself in the description.

"Let me tell you a story," Stanley said. "When I worked in the Pentagon the first time, I did a study about how we could keep better inventory of airplane repair parts as they moved from the manufacturer to Navy warehouses. I'd gone out and looked at some technology, new at the time, that the big package-shipping companies use now—hand-held scanning devices and all that jazz. I became an in-house expert of sorts.

"So one morning the admiral I work for tells me to go talk to this other staff about my work, because they're looking at a similar system and need some advice. I head over there with my little briefcase, thinking that I get to be the good guy, help somebody out. But the guy I'm supposed to brief attacks my work even before I start presenting, complaining about how the study was put together and how my data was flawed. So I'm already ticked off. Then his boss, another admiral, comes into the room, and the meeting starts. But I'm so focused on this guy's criticism—which was unfair—that I can't really concentrate. All I kept thinking was, 'You jerk. You must have some hidden agenda here. Why don't you want this project to succeed?' I used all my brain cells thinking about what this guy had said and how I was going to rebut, and I had none left to brief the admiral. As you can imagine, it wasn't a very impressive briefing.

"That same thing can happen when you're trying to listen to someone who's upset, or is attacking you or your decision. You use all your brainpower mounting a defense, or thinking about what a jerk that person is, and you have none left over to listen, to understand the person's position. You have to listen so that you can ask good questions."

Stanley stood, walked to the counter and picked up the coffee pot; Guy declined a refill.

"You said you've got to learn how to use the new capabilities pretty quickly, right?"

"Yeah, but I don't know what the new organization is going to look like. We're flying by the seat of our pants."

"Did you ask the people on your team? They might have some ideas. And, if they come up with the idea, they're more likely to get behind it when you're trying to make it happen. They'll own it."

"I wish I could get Wally over here for some coaching," Guy said. "But I doubt if he even knows he needs help."

Stanley put his empty coffee cup into the dishwasher.

"Do you know what … what's his real name?"

"J.W."

"Do you know what J.W. wants from you?"

"He wants me to impress this Hulton guy," Guy said. "But all he told me was to get everyone on the same sheet of music."

"It's frustrating when you're not sure what the boss wants, that's for sure. My question for you is: does your team know what you want?"

Guy didn't have an answer for that one. After a few quiet seconds, he said, "I'm not even sure I know what I want."

"Well, that's something, anyway," Stanley said, smiling. "It's not the million-dollar answer, but it is, at least, the million-dollar question."

"Thanks for the advice, and for the pruning hook," Guy said, standing and shaking Stanley's hand. "Any chance I could entice you to come into the city for a visit to Eaton, maybe a little leadership talk over lunch?"

"You buying?"

CHAPTER 2

The next Tuesday, Stanley showed up at 11 a.m. sharp, dressed in a blazer and tie, which was more formal, by several degrees, than anyone on Guy's floor. Guy showed his neighbor around, introducing him to any of the staff who looked up from their work. The men had to thread their way through a maze of editing consoles, rolling bookshelves and computer stands, and chairs stacked practically on top of one another.

Guy thought he'd skip introducing Stanley to Linda Hutchinson, who had appropriated a fairly good-sized chunk of floor space in a sunny corner, but she saw the men coming and approached them. She shook hands with Stanley, then turned to Guy and said, "Do you really expect us to work under these conditions?"

Guy looked around. The setup wasn't ideal, but no one else had complained.

"I'm used to having my own space, my own office, for that matter," Linda said, directing her comments to Stanley. "Here we're living in a commune."

"I asked about getting a second restroom up here," Guy said. "It's going to take awhile, and we have to get the landlord to make the modifications."

"Are we talking days? Weeks?" Linda asked.

"At least a month," Guy said.

She didn't take her eyes off him. "I guess that means we'll be crammed in here for at least that long."

"I think so," Guy said.

"Terrific. That's terrific." She held her hand out to Stanley. "Very nice to meet you," she said, and then walked off without saying anything else to Guy.

The two men left the building, walked to a small luncheonette only a block from the Eaton offices, and sat at a table beside a big window that looked out on Second Street. It was a brilliant, sunny day, but a steady wind rattled the glass.

"See what I mean about Linda?" Guy said, after they'd been seated and served. "Big fan of mine. She looks at me as if she's surprised I can get myself dressed in the morning."

"You'll get used to that when your daughter is a teenager," Stanley said. He carefully spooned hot soup from a small cup into his mouth.

"I really did ask about a new bathroom," Guy said. "I made an issue of it, in fact. I can see that it's crowded on the floor."

"That little scene wasn't about how crowded it is on the floor," Stanley said, wiping his mouth with a paper napkin. "It's not even about the bathroom.

"What was it about?" Stanley asked.

"What did she say to you?"

Stanley wasn't making idle chatter, and Guy didn't even mind being quizzed, especially if it helped him deal with Linda. Her attitude seemed to be infecting other members of the team.

"One bathroom isn't enough for fifteen people, especially when men and women have to share it."

"OK," Stanley said.

"She's also unhappy with how crowded the floor is, all that equipment shoved into one space."

"Anything else?"

Guy thought for a moment. "Those seem to be her two big complaints."

"Do you remember her saying, 'I used to have my own office'? I imagine that's what this is really about."

"But no one has an office on our floor."

"It's not about the physical space," Stanley said. "It's about what having an office represents. Did she run the show at her old company?"

"She was sort of the second-in-command of her team," Guy said.

"Did she think she was in line to be *el jefe*?"

"Probably."

"And that all got yanked away from her because her dopey former boss ran off to Shangri-La with a cheerleader."

"I see," Guy said.

"It's good that you see, and we can talk in a minute about what you might do about Linda. First, let's talk about what you should do about Guy."

"What do you mean?"

"Somebody as smart as you should have figured this out when you first met her," Stanley said. "In fact, you should have anticipated a problem."

"So I need to work on those listening skills, like in the story you told me about the Pentagon briefing."

"Bingo," Stanley said. Then, "You have a pen on you?"

Guy pulled a pen from his shirt pocket. Stanley slid a clean paper napkin across the table.

"Number one: listening."

Guy made a note. This was the leadership class he never had.

"What else did we talk about the other day?" Stanley asked him.

"Uh ... you asked me if I knew what Wally wanted, and I said no."

Stanley just nodded. Guy had learned in their first conversation that this meant there was more to the answer.

"And ..."

"I asked if you knew what J.W. wanted, and you said no. First of all, you should stop calling him Wally, unless you're going to call him that to his face."

"That's what I've always called him."

"You haven't always been in charge. If you mock the boss, you send a message to your team that you're the kind of person who will talk behind someone's back. They gotta figure it's only a matter of time before you're saying stuff about them."

"OK," Guy said, not quite convinced.

"You told me you didn't know what J.W. wanted, and I asked …"

"You asked if my team knew what I wanted," Guy said when prompted.

"Write that down," Stanley said.

Guy wrote, "WHAT DO I WANT?" on the napkin.

"Now let's talk about your team and your responsibilities. Do you have a job description? Something written down?"

"Nothing formal, no."

"So how do you see your job?"

"Well, my team has to create marketing strategies and then design and execute them, and I oversee that process. I make sure things are moving to completion, and I make sure the right people are working on the right projects."

"So you've got to accomplish the mission, to use a Navy term. Get the projects done on time and on budget, that kind of thing."

"Right."

"That it?"

Guy suspected that he was supposed to have more ideas for what his job entailed, but all he could think of at the moment was that he had to attend a lot of meetings with people who talked like John Hulton.

"I'm not sure," he said.

"OK. You said you put the right people on the right jobs. What do you mean by the right people?"

"Well, if I have a client who wants to set up a booth at a fancy trade show—I mean really wow 'em—I have two people who are really good at that."

"Are there other people who'd like to do that kind of stuff?"

"Sure," Guy answered. "It's one of the fun things to do. Plus you get to travel."

"So why not let more people do it?"

"I thought being efficient meant getting the best people on the task."

"A lot of the time it does. But efficiency isn't your only concern, or shouldn't be your only concern," Stanley said. "Tell me, do those two conference booth people get to do other stuff, like work on the overall marketing campaign?"

"Not very often. We're usually on a tight schedule to get this stuff done, and so I use these two because they get it done fast and they do a good job."

"What if they quit tomorrow?"

"I'd be in trouble," Guy said.

"It's good to let people work in areas in which they do well," Stanley offered. "When people are successful at their work, they can be happy. But keeping people in one area with no chance to move, or excluding other people because you don't want to take the time for them to learn, those are bad ideas. You've got to find a balance between putting people where they'll succeed and helping them stretch their capabilities a little bit."

"So I should give conference work to people who haven't done it before?"

"I'd say you should let someone who hasn't done it before, but who has expressed an interest, sit in on a couple of work sessions with the experts. That would give your conference people a chance to learn how to teach, and it would let other people have a shot at the fun jobs."

Guy looked down at the table, where he'd spread two napkins. On one, he'd written "LISTENING" and "WHAT DO I WANT?" On the other, he'd written "JOB DESCRIPTION" but nothing else.

"What do you call that? Letting people learn different jobs?"

"Put that under the heading 'Development,'" Stanley said. "You've got to develop your people. That's part of motivating them, and it's also part of improving the team."

"I have a young guy named Peter who wants a role in this new project for Concord."

"And how ready is he?"

"Good question. I'd probably be able to answer that better if I knew exactly what the project was going to entail, but we're still in the early stages."

Talking about Peter and the Concord project reminded Guy that he had not been able to set up a meeting with John Hulton's "people," though it had been a week. He had managed a series of brief phone calls that helped him to learn a bit more about what Hulton wanted.

Hulton's company, Concord Home, had started out as a mortgage company in Massachusetts but had been moving steadily to build a national brand in the fragmented world of home lending. Hulton had plans to streamline the process of securing a home loan, then to take his process nationwide. He was going to move into home lending with a simplified model, in the same manner that McDonald's had standardized French fries across the country, the same way that a Florida Holiday Inn resembled an Oregon Holiday Inn. Concord's business had huge potential, and Wally Eaton intended to ride it all the way.

When Concord's sales force gathered in Philadelphia just before Christmas to learn how they were to sell in the coming year, they expected to be handed a master plan and all the dazzling techno tools they could use. The problem was that none of those tools existed, because there was no strategy yet. The whole thing gave Guy a headache.

Guy wrote "DEVELOPMENT," then, below that, put "IMPROVE TEAM." The writing was bleeding through the napkin and becoming illegible.

Stanley looked at the notes and said, "We should get you some paper and get a little more organized about this."

Guy paid the check and the two men walked back to the office, but instead of going up to the second floor, Guy led Stanley into the first-floor conference room. The long table that dominated the room held a telephone and a stack of legal pads. The walls were decorated with lithographs of golf fairways. Stanley took a seat, and Guy shut the door behind them. Every once in a while, someone walked to the door and peered through the glass panel at the two men, but no one interrupted.

"Let's talk about your job first, in a large sense," Stanley said.

Guy held the tablet in front of him. He had the same feeling he'd had in school when, early in a semester, he figured out that he'd landed with a professor who had a lot to teach him.

"What is leadership?" Stanley asked.

Guy laughed. "Boy, you weren't kidding when you said we're talking in the large sense." Then, "Let's see. I guess leadership is when you get other people to do things."

"What things?"

"Uh … the things you want them to do?"

"Good," Stanley said. "Dwight Eisenhower said that leadership is when other people do what you want them to do *because they want to do it.*"

"I'm not sure I follow," Guy said.

"Well, there are three kinds of leadership," Stanley said.

Guy began writing.

"There's leadership from authority: the do-this-or-I'll-break-your-legs kind. Then there's leadership through motivation: the do-this-and-I'll-give-you-that kind. Then there's inspirational leadership: that's where people buy into the leader's plan and the organization's goals, and they do things because they really want to do them."

"And that's the best kind, right?"

"Well, there are times and places for all of these things, but in your situation, leading a bunch of talented people who are pretty much free-thinkers, yeah, I'd say that's what you should shoot for."

Stanley stood and walked to a whiteboard that hung on a sidewall. He erased a column of numbers, picked up a marker and wrote "LEADERSHIP" near the top. Below that, he stacked a few small circles for some bullet points. Beside the circles he wrote:

- INFLUENCE
- OPERATE
- IMPROVE

"OK," he said, putting the cap on the pen and turning to Guy. "A leader has to influence people, operate to accomplish the mission, and improve the organization, *capisce?*"

"Ka-what?"

"*Capisce.* It means, 'Do you understand?' If you do, you say, *capisco.*"

The reply didn't sound quite as authentic coming from Guy, an Ohio native, but Stanley smiled.

"OK," Stanley continued, "Influence means you gotta provide ..."

He wrote "PURPOSE, DIRECTION, MOTIVATION" beside the first bullet point.

"What do you think this means?" he asked, tapping the board next to "PURPOSE."

"They have to know why they're doing something?"

"Sure. And it would be helpful if your people also thought that it was a good idea or for a worthwhile cause, whether that's having the best ship in the fleet or having the most satisfied customers."

"My team likes it when a customer is blown away by a concept we develop, when we get a lot of 'That was GREAT!' kind of comments."

"Good. How about this?" Stanley asked, pointing at "DIRECTION."

"That means you have to tell them what to do."

"Not exactly, or at least not in every case," the older man explained. "I mean, if you have someone who's really experienced at identifying target markets or preparing print work, you're not going to give them detailed instructions about how to do that, right?"

"That would insult them," Guy said.

"Right. That's micromanaging. For most people, it's better to tell them what you want to have happen and let them figure out how to get it done. Obviously, this is a sliding scale. The most inexperienced team members need more guidance than the most experienced, and chances are that everyone else falls somewhere in between. Your job is to figure out how much guidance to give."

"So you can give enough," Guy said as he wrote.

"So you can give them just enough so that they're challenged. It's like you're always putting things just beyond their grasp. That's how people learn."

"How about this one? 'MOTIVATION.'"

"That's a big one, isn't it?" Guy said.

"Absolutely. What do you think motivates people? Why do people work? More important, why do they work hard, stay an extra hour, put in a little more effort to really nail something?"

"Money?"

"Actually, most surveys show that employees rank money way down the list of what they're looking for."

Guy looked a little skeptical.

"Did you get a raise with your new responsibilities?"

"Yeah. Melanie and I went out to celebrate. Had a nice dinner in a restaurant that didn't give out crayons with the place mats."

"So the extra few bucks was the margin of your being happy or unhappy?"

"No, I guess not," Guy said. "I guess it was more the fact that the promotion and the raise meant that people recognized my work was worth something, or something more, in this case."

"Right," Stanley said. "Workers always rank recognition above pay when they talk about what makes them happy at work. They also rank autonomy higher than money. People want to have control over what they do."

"So if I give someone a project but let them figure out the details of how to do it, they have more autonomy than if I dictate every little facet, right?"

"Now you're getting it," Stanley said. "There's more to it than that, of course, but you're grasping the basics."

Just as Guy was starting to feel pleased with himself, he saw Linda Hutchinson's face at the window beside the door. He smiled at her, but she didn't smile back. Guy hoped she'd go away, but Stanley opened the door and greeted her warmly.

"Hello, Linda," he said, as if finding her staring through the glass was a splendid surprise. "Would you like to join us?"

"What are you guys doing?" she asked, without crossing the threshold into the room.

"Having a little chat about leadership. It would be great if you could join us."

Linda marched into the room, but the look on her face, Guy thought, was more about what she could teach them than what she might learn from them.

"I'm sure Guy has a lot to teach us all," she said, as if Guy weren't in the room.

"We were just talking about what motivates people," Stanley explained.

"Being treated with respect," she said. "Not getting herded around like cattle with no explanation."

Guy looked down at the tablet. He had been enjoying the little class Stanley was running, but all that had changed when Miss Passive-Aggressive came through the door.

"I couldn't agree with you more," Stanley said.

Guy looked up to see if Stanley was being sarcastic. The older man looked completely sincere. *The traitor*, Guy thought.

"So what—specifically—is bugging you?" Stanley asked. There was nothing confrontational in his voice; he was being completely charming. In fact, Guy thought the old sailor might just be flirting with the younger woman.

Linda counted on her fingers as she spoke. "No bathroom. No place to work; all the equipment crowded onto the floor. No one has told us exactly what we're going to be doing here. Now I have Peter, who looks just old enough to rush a fraternity, telling me that he's going to *bring me on board* on a project he's working on."

A little warning light went off in Guy's head. He'd have to warn Peter to approach Linda with some tact.

"What else?" Stanley asked.

Linda's voice lost some of its stridency.

"I guess ... I guess I'm still a little ticked off about what happened to my company, Kensington, with that clown, my old boss, running off with all our money and that bimbo."

"That would get to me," Stanley said. "Would that get to you, Guy?"

"Yep," Guy said, petulantly.

"And I understand you went from being in charge, or at least second in line, to ... what's your position here?"

"That's a good question," Linda said, with a little too much enthusiasm. She turned to Guy. "I can't really say what my position is here."

"We were just saying how much Guy needs your help rolling your team into this unit, making the most of what everyone is capable of."

Linda looked at Stanley for signs that he was mocking her. When she was convinced he was sincere, she said, "I have a couple of ideas."

"I want to hear them," Guy said. "I could use the help."

Linda watched him for a silent moment, then smiled at Guy for the first time.

"I'll be ready to give you some ideas tomorrow," she said. "Give me the rest of the day to flesh them out."

When she was gone, Guy said, "That went surprisingly well."

"Under 'MOTIVATION,' make a note about listening," Stanley said. "All she wanted to do was be heard, and you've been avoiding her."

"Like the plague," Guy admitted.

Stanley laughed. "Know what the real kick in the pants is going to be? I'll bet she comes up with some really good ideas, and you wind up adopting some of them."

He turned back to the whiteboard. "What about this one?" he asked, pointing to the last bullet point, "OPERATE."

"I guess that means you've got to get the job done. Make your numbers, finish your projects, keep your customers happy."

"You've got to do all of that," Stanley said, "and you've got to do it in line with your personal values and the company values.

"That leaves us with 'IMPROVE.'"

"You said that meant improve the organization," Guy said.

"Right. It should be in better shape when you leave than when you came on board. You improve the organization by working on the systems, but also by improving the individuals. That's development. You've got to invest in training, but you've also got to look for ways to keep people challenged, look for new jobs that will stretch their abilities. You've got to think about what the next challenge is for each person. It will be like juggling a bunch of different lesson plans in your head."

Stanley capped the marker and dropped it into the tray below the board.

"Remember the million-dollar question?"

"Sure," Guy said. "What do I want from my team?"

"If you could tell them that, it would give them a real head start on how to work for you."

"So I have to go through a planning cycle, figure out the business objectives, all that stuff?"

"Eventually, but that's not what I'm talking about right now. I'm talking about more general stuff. You've got to let your team know what you believe in, what's important to you, how you want to operate. In a way, it's like giving them a look at the compass inside you, the thing that keeps you on course.

"From that, you can derive other stuff: what you should do on a day-to-day basis. And if you tell them what to expect, they can hold you to it."

"I don't know that I've ever sat down and tried to articulate something as broad as 'what I believe in,'" Guy said.

"That puts you in the majority," Stanley said. "But if you do it, if you develop a leadership philosophy, you'll have a strong foundation for the decisions you make, for how you interact with people. And if you stick with it, your people will see that you're consistent. Nothing ruins morale on a team faster than a boss who says one thing and does another."

"I agree with that," Guy said. "Wally, I mean J.W., is a great one for making grand announcements about some new direction the company is going to take or changes he's going to institute. Then he goes back to the old way or does something completely different, and everyone is disappointed and angry."

"What do you know about leadership?" Stanley asked. "What do you believe?"

"Talk about your open-ended questions."

Stanley laughed. "Just tell me a story. Part of your job as a leader is to be a teacher. Good teachers tell stories."

"You mean, make something up?"

"If necessary," Stanley said. "But what I'm really getting at is that if you use a story—if you create a beginning, middle, and end, if you talk about people and actions instead of concepts and theories, people will understand you more easily and they'll remember what you told them."

"Why is that?"

Stanley leaned back in his chair and put his hands behind his head, fingers interlaced.

"What did the three little pigs use to build their houses?"

Guy paused, to see if it was a joke. Then he answered, "Straw, sticks, and bricks."

"And what was the moral?"

"Put the work in to do things right the first time," Guy said.

"See? People remember stories."

"So how do I go about creating this leadership philosophy?" Guy asked.

"We can tackle that later," Stanley said. "But here's your homework."

He reached across the table, took Guy's legal pad, and turned to a blank page, where he drew a line from top to bottom, right down the middle. At the top of the left column, he wrote "BEST" and at the top of the other, he wrote "WORST."

"Over the next day or so, I want you to think of the best leader you've ever worked for, and I want you to write down what made that person the best. Then I want you to think of the worst leader you've ever worked for, and I want you to write down what made that person so bad."

"You mean, what they did that made them so bad?"

"What they did, what their values were, what kind of skills they had, both technical and interpersonal. When you finish that, we'll talk some more," Stanley said. He stood and buttoned his blazer. Guy walked him to the door.

"Thanks for coming," Guy said. "I learned a lot today."

"Good," Stanley said, putting on his overcoat. "I like teaching, so this was fun for me, too. I'm going to dig around in my papers when I get home. I have something to show you that may help."

"What's that?"

"Well, I went through this drill—writing a leadership philosophy—a number of times when I was in the Navy, and I'm sure I still have my notes and stuff. We'll look at them together."

Guy stopped by Ellen Grady's office on the first floor, next to the conference room. The CFO was looking at her computer screen and had her back to the open door when Guy knocked.

"You look pretty chipper," she said, turning after he greeted her.

"I just spent an hour with a neighbor of mine, talking about leadership, and I'm pretty sure I learned more than I have over the past ten years."

"Oh? What did you learn?"

"Well, for starters, I learned that I've got to let my team know what I want from them. And I'm not just talking about projects and deadlines, but bigger stuff, too, like my definition of good performance."

"Sounds reasonable," Ellen said.

"Do you do that?"

"Something like that, I guess. I used to be a professor, taught accounting for a few years before coming over to business. On the first day of class every semester, I let my students know where I stood. You know, all the predictable stuff: you've got to come to class; hand in your work on time; don't copy someone else's work; don't come whining to me asking for help the day before the exam, if I haven't seen you all semester. That kind of stuff."

"Were you a tough prof?" Guy asked.

"I guess so," Ellen said. "But they all knew that from the beginning. I didn't hide the fact that I was tough. If you signed up for my course, you knew what you were getting into. You worked hard, and you learned a lot."

"A lot of the guys I played ball with spent hours trying to find out who the easiest profs were, especially for courses they took during football season."

"If you think about it, that's actually pretty logical," Ellen said. "I mean, if their main concern was a good football season, they were just trying to focus."

"You think?" Guy asked, smiling.

"I think most people want to succeed. How often do you meet someone who deliberately sets out to fail at something? There are plenty of people who want it to come easily, and there are loads of people who aren't willing to do what it takes to succeed, but I really believe that most people want to do well. In my courses, I worked off that assumption."

"Meaning?" Guy asked.

"You come in wanting to do well, and I tell you what it will take. I can't make it any more fair than that."

"That goes along with what Stanley was telling me a little while ago. It's better to let people know exactly what you want from them."

"Stanley sounds like a smart guy," Ellen said. "I found some other benefits, too. If I had to articulate what I wanted, what I thought was important, that helped keep me on course, too. I was more likely to make consistent decisions."

"He talked about something very similar, called it a 'compass,' like on a ship. It's surprising how much of his experience in the Navy applies here," Guy said before heading upstairs to do his homework.

The mess on the second floor had been cleared, and everyone was engaged in some sort of work, so things were pretty quiet. The folks who'd moved from Kensington were cleaning up some projects they'd brought over, and all of Guy's people had their heads down, working. Guy sat at his desk and spread the piece of paper with the BEST and WORST columns in front of him. He wrote "Hadley" on the BEST side.

Mark Hadley had been the linebacker coach at Notre Dame for the four years that Guy played that position; his was the name that came to mind immediately when Stanley asked about the best leader Guy had known.

Guy tapped the point of his pencil on the paper, and then wrote "concern for people" on the first line. Coach Hadley knew his players: knew which freshmen were homesick, who had a bruised muscle and needed more rest, who was sick, who was having difficulty in class. Guy knew that football players were treated like interchangeable parts in many big programs, but Hadley always treated his players like they were his own sons. Not that he was easy on them ...

He wrote "tough" on the next line.

Guy had shown up in South Bend with a bit of an attitude, as if he was doing the team a favor by putting on the green and gold jersey. He'd been a high school All-American, and, truth be told, he thought he was going to make the team easily and be a star. On the field, his attitude translated to: *I'll hustle when I have a chance to shine, to get some individual recognition. Otherwise, I'm saving myself.*

Guy remembered a practice, on a blistering August afternoon of his freshman year, when he half-stepped through a play because the runner was hit right at the line of scrimmage, and it didn't look like he needed to help with the tackle. Guy had taken two quick steps toward the ball carrier, and then slowed when he heard the solid crack of pads that meant the linemen had made the tackle.

Coach Hadley appeared at Guy's elbow, screaming as if his hair were on fire.

"*What are you doing?*" he wanted to know.

"The linemen made the stop," Guy had said, a little uncertain.

"The linemen made a hit, but until that ball carrier is on the ground and you hear a whistle, I want you chasing him down like your life depended on it. You got that? Every play, every play, every play!"

For the next two weeks, Hadley seemed to be at Guy's side, or in his face, or screaming in his ear, at every moment of the long practices. At first Guy was amused, then he was bothered, and finally—after he felt he was doing as much running as he could—he was annoyed with the coach.

That's when Hadley called him in for a meeting. Guy was terrified that he was about to be cut, but Hadley was cool and friendly, inviting Guy to take a seat, offering him a bottle of water. Then the coach put a question to his young player.

"Do you want to succeed here?"

"Yes," Guy answered.

Then the coach explained exactly what that would take. When he finished, he asked if Guy had any questions, but he'd been so clear that there was no room for misinterpretation. Finally, Hadley told Guy, "You have a lot of potential. I suspect that, up to this point, you've done well on size and speed and natural talent. But this is college ball, and there are whole squads of players with your size and speed. You can be good, but you've got to work at it, and that starts with hustling—all out— on every play."

No one had ever explained things to Guy like that before, and it changed his entire approach to football. His teammates started calling him Mister Hustle, and he could count on one hand the number of times in the next four years that Coach Hadley had to yell at him. After graduation, when he questioned whether or not he should take a shot as a walk-on with the pros, he'd called Coach Hadley, and his mentor spent over an hour on the phone with him, helping him sort out what he wanted from what he felt pressured to do.

Guy wrote "fair" on the third line. Hadley did not play favorites when it came to determining who would start, who would get the most playing time. If you hustled and got results, you played. He'd bench a big-name scholarship player as fast as he'd bench a walk-on.

"Sportsmanship" went on the next line. Guy remembered Hadley asking one trash-talking player if he'd say all those things if his mother were in the stands and could hear him.

Guy put "respect" and "do the right thing" on the next two lines.

During Guy's junior year, word reached the coaches that one of their star players had shoved his girlfriend around at a party. Hadley confronted the young man. At first the player tried to dismiss the story as a rumor, then he tried to make light of it, as if it were no big deal.

"You can turn yourself in to the campus police, or I'll do it for you," Hadley told the player. When the young man was suspended from the team, powerful alumni started screaming for Hadley's head. Because the girl hadn't pressed charges, some of the players thought that Hadley was sticking his nose in when he didn't need to. At a team meeting, he stood on a chair and explained himself in a few sentences.

"How many people here learned, probably in kindergarten, that you shouldn't hit people? Especially that big boys like you fellas shouldn't hit girls?"

When it became obvious that it wasn't a rhetorical question, the big players started raising their hands.

"Wrong then," Hadley said, "wrong now." Then he climbed off the chair and left the room.

Guy smiled to himself and wrote "clear standards" in the Coach Hadley column. Then, at the top of the WORST column, he started to write "J.W." but thought better of it and left the name off. No telling who might see his notes.

The first thing that came to mind was the fact that J.W. was late to his own meetings. Guy wrote "inconsiderate, rude" at the top of the column. J.W. often forgot the names of employees, and after meeting Melanie for the third or fourth time, he held out his hand and said, "I don't believe we've met."

J.W. also had a habit of taking credit for the firm's work, as if no one else were involved in any of the projects. Guy often heard him use the word "I"—as in "I really had fun putting this campaign together"—when talking to clients.

J.W. also refused to deal with poor performers, or even to confront unpleasant situations. In a small company like Eaton, it was easy to see who was pulling his or her weight, and who wasn't. Just a year earlier, it became clear to almost everyone that a key member of the sales team was spending his time trying to sell his services as a consultant to Eaton's clients. J.W. refused even to discuss the situation and instead waited until the man left on his own. During the eight or nine months the man was doing his own work instead of what he was supposed to be doing, the sales forces had to carry the extra load, which just about ruined morale. When J.W. announced that there'd be a going-away party for the departing salesman, there was almost a mutiny on the first floor, and J.W. allowed the party to be canceled. He never did talk to the disenchanted sales team.

Guy looked up from his sheet and watched the people on his team. Peter, the ponytailed latte drinker, sat directly in Guy's line of sight.

A week had passed since they first heard of the Concord project, and Guy was impressed with how Peter had jumped into the work. Apparently Peter had more luck than Guy in getting the Concord folks to fill him in on their ideas for marketing their new approach to home mortgages, because he told Guy repeatedly that things were "moving along nicely." All things considered, Guy was happy that he'd given Peter the challenge and that Stanley's advice about how to develop leaders seemed to confirm what he was doing.

Maybe this leadership stuff isn't so difficult after all, he thought. Stanley had told him to take a week to make his list of good and bad leadership traits, but Guy thought he was ready to move forward.

"You're still in the fast reading group, Cedrick," he told himself.

Guy stopped at the big electronics warehouse store on the way home, as he had done twice in the last six weeks, to eyeball a big-screen television. The model he coveted had a flat screen framed in silver and a sharp picture that, when it was tuned to a sports channel, was so clear that he felt as if he were back on the field, suited up and waiting for the opening kickoff. The television would just fit in the entertainment center that dominated one corner of the family room, Guy had figured after careful measurement. It would not fit, Melanie had pointed out at least four times in the last month, in their tight household budget.

Melanie, who had been an accountant before taking off for a few years to stay home with their daughter, handled the family's money. Guy was happy to hand over the job, because he had no confidence in his own ability to keep track of what was coming in and what was going out. Melanie insisted that he sit down with her every month or two and go over their goals and objectives, but that had evolved from a conversation in which they both participated into more of a briefing, in which Melanie told him what was going on, and asked for his input. Guy had grown increasingly quiet during these discussions, not because Melanie excluded him, but because he wanted to be excluded. In fact, if Melanie made all the budget decisions, he'd be perfectly content.

"I'm not doing this all myself," she told him one Saturday afternoon after he'd sat, mostly silent, as she explained her plan for putting away money for the new roof they'd need within a year.

"I do other stuff by myself," Guy told her. "Division of labor is more efficient, right?"

"It isn't the labor that has me concerned," she told him. "This stuff is important, and we both need to be in on the decisions. I don't mind doing the grunt work, but I don't want to sit around making up fiscal policy. This has to be a partnership."

That all made sense to Guy, of course. It was rational and enlightened and made his wife happy. He loved Melanie more than he would have thought possible, and he honestly believed that he was carrying his share of the load in planning when he calculated the price of the television—twenty-one hundred dollars—against the raise he expected this year, but Melanie was uncomfortable with debt for the sake of what she called "consumer toys," and he wanted to be a considerate husband.

Guy pulled his cell phone from his pocket and punched the speed-dial for home. He got the machine but didn't leave a message. It'd be more fun to surprise her.

"This one," he told the first salesman to come within hailing distance. "Free delivery, right?"

It was over in a couple of minutes: a quick swipe of the credit card, directions to his house for the delivery driver, and Guy was standing by the store's front door, buttoning his overcoat and thinking about the upcoming college bowl season. On the way home he whistled various fight songs and planned a big party for the Bowl Championship Series: lots of beer and maybe one of those six-foot hoagies that came strapped to a slice of plywood. He made one quick stop, then home; Melanie's car was in the driveway when he pulled up.

He found her in the kitchen and handed her the bouquet of flowers he'd picked up just around the corner. She smiled and pulled him down by the neck to kiss him on the lips. Donna, their four-year-old, squeezed in between them as she often did when they hugged, and patted Guy's legs with her little hands until he pulled her up. Guy walked into the family room with Donna perched on his shoulder.

In a cheerful voice, the kind he used to read bedtime stories to Donna, he asked his little girl, "Sweetie, aren't you excited about the college Bowl Championship Series?"

For an answer, Donna stuck her finger into Guy's ear. He pulled his head back, watching Melanie out of the corner of his eye, but she didn't look up from the counter, where she was trimming the flowers for a glass vase.

Gotta raise the cuteness factor, he thought.

He held Donna above his head, then shifted her tiny weight until she was over his right shoulder.

"FIGHTING ..." he said.

"EYE-RSHHH!" the little girl squealed, as her dad flipped her easily to his other hand, over his left shoulder. They'd been playing this game, in season and out, since she was a toddler.

"FIGHTING!"

"EYE-RSHHH!"

Melanie looked up, smiling.

"I bought that big TV today," he said cheerily, as if it had been a great accomplishment, the hunter home with his kill.

Melanie cocked her head to one side, not quite sure of what she'd heard. "What was that?"

"That big TV we've been looking at. I bought it today. Remember, we talked about it last weekend?"

"We talked about it," she said. "We didn't agree that we'd buy it."

"Honey, you know that I've had my eye on that, and I wanted to get it before the bowl season. I told you I was going to stop by the store again this week."

"So? 'Stopping by the store' is not the same as 'I'm stopping by the store to spend two thousand dollars on a television,' as far as I can tell."

"Why did you think I was stopping? I wasn't just going to stand around admiring it."

"What you do in the store is your business," she said, a little more sharply. "What you bring home from the store is our business, and stuff that's our business requires some discussion, I think. Aren't those the rules we've been playing by?"

"We did discuss it," Guy said, setting Donna on the floor. "And I thought we agreed on it."

"How in the world could you think that?" Melanie actually had her hands on her hips. Guy considered it a quirk of their relationship that he found her especially attractive when she was angry about something. Fortunately, she didn't have to be angry with him for the spell to work.

"Look, I can call them up and cancel the delivery, if that's what you want."

"This isn't about the television, Guy."

"It isn't?" he said, genuinely surprised.

"Of course it isn't. This is about the fact that you don't understand what agreement looks like. And it's about the fact that you don't want to help me make budget decisions, but you go out and spend the money, and then you expect me to just clean up the mess and make everything work."

"It isn't as if I don't make a contribution," he said. "I'm working my butt off, and I'm about to get a raise."

"I'm not disputing that at all," Melanie said. "I'm saying that we have to reach these kinds of big decisions together."

"Is it so wrong that I want something every once in a while?"

"What about what I want?"

"You want a big TV? You want something else? I never put any restrictions on what you spend."

"You're missing the point entirely," Melanie said. "Keep the TV, don't keep the TV, I don't really care. What I care about right now is how we got to this point of buying the stupid TV."

"I just did it," Guy said, smiling. "You know, like the commercial says."

He was ready for another round, ready to start talking about the TV as if it had already been delivered and paid for. He was confident that once he had it in the house, it would stay in the house.

But Melanie just said, "Very funny," turned on her heel, and left the room.

CHAPTER 3

As soon as Guy walked into his neighbor's house, Stanley asked what was wrong; he could read it on the younger man's face. Guy told Stanley that he'd had a run-in with Melanie.

"Did you and your wife ever fight about money?" Guy asked Stanley. They were in Stanley's study, which had several handsome prints of Navy ships, and a small, very shiny brass bell on a side table. The replica of a ship's bell had been given to Stanley by his crew when he gave up command of his last ship.

"We used to stress about money," Stanley said. "Especially when the kids were young and there really wasn't enough to go around."

"I read somewhere that fights about money are one of the main reasons people get divorced," Guy said. When he felt Stanley looking at him, he added, "Not that Melanie and I are in any danger of splitting up. She's my best friend, and we hardly ever disagree. When we do, it really eats at me, and I know it eats at her, too."

"So what are you going to do to fix it?"

"I canceled the order for the big TV I bought," Guy said. "But that only made me feel worse, and it didn't seem to help her much either." He recounted the conversation for Stanley, who summarized it neatly.

"Sending the TV back didn't make her happy because that's not what she wanted. She doesn't want you to go without the TV, and she isn't keeping score on who 'wins' what argument. It sounds like she wants you guys to be on the same side."

"What do you mean?"

"You want the same things?"

"No. I wanted a big screen TV, and she didn't."

Stanley laughed, and Guy had the feeling he'd missed the joke.

"Try to get your mind off the TV for a minute, OK? When I ask if you guys want the same things, I'm talking about respect, affection, a good home for your kids, an education for your daughter, that kind of stuff."

"Yeah, sure. I mean, I guess so. We never really sat down and talked about it in those exact terms," Guy said.

"This thing we're doing to help you clarify your leadership philosophy can help in your personal life, too," Stanley said.

When Guy didn't answer, the older man continued.

"What do you think Melanie wants out of your conversations about money?"

"She wants to let me know where we stand," Guy said. Then, thinking about her other comments, he added, "And she wants me to be involved in the decisions."

"Why?"

"Because she thinks ... no, she really believes, that we have to be partners. Equal partners when it comes to big stuff."

"Why does she care about managing the money?"

"So that we can accomplish our goals, I guess. Like you said, send the kids to college, pay the mortgage."

"So security is part of this. And she wants you as a partner so that you don't resent the decisions she makes. Maybe also because she thinks that the two of you can make better decisions than she can alone."

"Like the solo move I made on the TV."

"You're allowed to lose your mind every once in a while," Stanley said. "But that will happen less often if you know exactly where Melanie is coming from and what she wants, and if she knows the same about you."

"So when you were in the Navy, did you moonlight as a marriage counselor?"

"Sort of. In all those years of dealing with sailors who had to spend long periods of time away from home, I probably heard every conceivable hard luck story."

"You got involved with people's personal lives?" Guy asked.

"The military is more paternalistic than most civilian organizations," Stanley answered. "When we say 'take care of people,' we're really talking about the whole package, on-duty and off. Besides, if you take some twenty-one-year-old newlywed away from his wife, or away from her husband, it's going to have an effect on that sailor's work. Only an idiot would ignore that aspect of leadership.

"Does the good leader on your list show any interest in people's lives?"

Guy looked at the entries under Coach Hadley's name. "First thing on the list, in fact, is 'concern for people.'"

Guy told Stanley a couple of stories about Coach Hadley, including the less-than-flattering portrait of himself as a cocky freshman who thought he was too good for the program.

"It doesn't sound like he was overly concerned about being buddies with the players."

Guy laughed. "No, he was more likely to kick you in the tail than he was to hold your hand."

"So he balanced concern and compassion with a drive to get the job done," Stanley said.

"Yeah, but it was more than that," Guy said. "He wanted to get the job done, and he was willing to teach us, to invest time in us so that we learned. And he even went further than that. I always felt he had a better handle on what I was capable of than I did. He could see potential on the other side of a lot of hard work. He not only pushed me through the work, but he also painted a picture for me, showed me what I could be like if I were willing to keep at it."

"That's a great description," Stanley said. "Take a minute to write that down."

Guy made some notes; then Stanley asked about his worst leader.

"Any sign of that kind of interest in the worst leader you identified?"

"Not really. He's concerned with himself, with how he looks, with taking credit. And he certainly doesn't invest the time in learning about people, at least not the way Coach Hadley did.

"The other thing about Coach Hadley was that he wasn't afraid to do what was right, or what he believed was right."

Guy told Stanley the story about the player who had shoved his girlfriend and about Coach Hadley's explanation: it was wrong in kindergarten; it was still wrong. Stanley laughed out loud.

"I'd love to meet this guy," he said.

"He retired a few years ago, but you can see him on the sidelines at the home games."

"So he had a sense of right and wrong. Where do you suppose that came from?" Stanley asked. "Where does anyone get a sense of what's right?"

"Well, Coach Hadley said he got it, or at least part of it, in kindergarten. I suppose we develop our sense of right and wrong from a combination of things: our home life, our schooling, our experiences, any religious education."

"What about in an organization?" Stanley asked.

"I guess in an organization, a leader has to adopt the values of the organization and build from there. I imagine you had certain values that, if they weren't peculiar to the Navy, were at least common to Navy people, right?"

"Exactly. The Navy talks about loyalty, and always uses the word 'shipmate' when talking about personal loyalty.

"Does your company have clearly articulated values?" Stanley asked.

"Not that I'm aware of," Guy said. "Which means no, I guess. Hardly does any good if we have them written down somewhere and no one knows what they are."

"Does the person on the 'worst' side of your paper have any values that are obvious, whether they're good or bad?"

"I'm not really sure. Most of what I can tell you would describe his actions, and most of those are just selfish. But I'm not sure I could tell you what's important to him, other than himself, his golf game and his money."

"That tells me a lot, actually," Stanley said. If he suspected they were talking about J.W., he wasn't letting on. "It says something about you, too. About what you think is important in a leader."

"What do you mean?"

"A lot of what you wrote has to do with how the leader interacts with subordinates," Stanley said, looking over Guy's columns. "There's some stuff here about the results the organization achieves, less about the client. Any idea why that is? Why your thinking runs in those lines?"

Guy considered a print of an aircraft carrier on the wall beside where he sat. The ship was backlit in yellow light, as if dusk were approaching, and two jets drew straight lines parallel to the surface of the ocean.

"I guess I believe that if the leader gets the stuff right with the people who work for him, the other stuff will follow. Not automatically, but at least more naturally."

"In other words, one of the keys to having happy customers is having happy employees?" Stanley asked.

"Yeah, I guess I'd sign that," Guy said.

"All right," Stanley said. "By the way, there's no single answer to this stuff. Much of it is a matter of your personal philosophy, your own take on how things work."

"Isn't that relativism?" Guy asked. "What I believe about leadership is OK for me and my organization, and whatever you believe is OK for you and yours? I mean, Josef Stalin believed that terrorizing people, leading through fear, was OK. So is that defensible if he were here to say, 'That's just my philosophy'?"

"No," Stanley answered. "Because your philosophy still has to stand up to a bunch of tests: Will people follow you? And is it consistent with your values and the values of the organization? Finally, is it ethical?"

"That's a word you hear a lot," Guy said. "All the business schools are always talking about ethics every time some CEO gets locked up for fraud or stock manipulation or insider trading, but I'm not sure I know exactly what it means."

"Do you believe some things are right and other things are wrong, period, no room for discussion?"

When Guy didn't answer right away, Stanley said, "Pedophilia. Exploiting children in the sex industry. Wrong or right?"

"Wrong."

"OK. So we've just established that you believe some things are absolutes. We haven't drawn up an all-inclusive list yet, but we have something to start with.

"What you believe about right and wrong informs how you make decisions on a day-to-day basis. Moving from a very general rule—'stealing is wrong,' for instance—to a specific decision is called moral reasoning."

"But people won't always agree to the same interpretation, right?" Guy asked.

"Of course not. On the other hand, just because we can rationalize behavior doesn't mean we should.

"I remember reading this article," Stanley continued, "about a debate they had at some famous business school, when the faculty was considering whether or not to teach ethics. There were a bunch of professors in the room, all of them awash in learning, and they couldn't come to the most basic agreement about how to approach questions of right and wrong, or whether a business school should even be in that business. If it wasn't so sad, it would have made me laugh: a bunch of pointy-headed academics, with about a million years of college among them, and they couldn't reach a point that my mother, with her eighth-grade education, could have made for them in a minute or two. Some things are right, and some things are wrong, so it's OK to have a discussion about what those things are. It's a little like your coach getting up on a chair and asking the guys if they'd learned in kindergarten that it was wrong to push and hit people. 'Wrong then; wrong now.'

"I learned something very early in my career about leaders and the responsibility to make the call," Stanley said. "I was a midshipman at the academy, and I was conducting a haircut inspection. So we had the company lined up, and I'm walking through the ranks, checking haircuts and uniforms, all that stuff. And my company officer, a Marine named Cipriotti, is sort of walking through the ranks nearby, chatting up some of the mids. Cipriotti had been a corporal in the Korean War; by the time I knew him, he was a captain, assigned to the academy to teach mids about leadership.

"So I go up to this one mid, and his hair looks a little long to me, so I ask him, 'Did you get a haircut this week?' And he says yes, and I wind up looking at his hair for a while, then letting it slide.

"Later, Cipriotti comes up to me and says, 'Who the hell was running that inspection, you or the guy in ranks?' And I said, 'I was, sir.' But it comes out like a question, like, 'I was? Sir?'"

Stanley laughed at himself and at the memory.

"'So why did you ask him if he got a haircut?' Cipriotti wanted to know. 'His hair was either in regulation or not. He doesn't make that call. You do. And if I can't get you to make a simple call like that—*your hair is too long or your hair is OK*—how am I going to trust you with a ship, or a company of Marines?'

"Get it?" Stanley asked Guy.

"I think so."

"You get paid the big bucks to make the hard calls," Stanley said. "OK, enough hundred-year-old Navy stories. It's time for you to write a short description of a good leader and a short description of a bad leader. Don't just describe the one person in each column, but broaden your thinking a little bit to include other good leaders you've known. Keep it brief. Take U.S. Grant's advice on writing: 'Write as if sending a telegram to a fool, which will be prepaid by a miser.'"

Stanley stood up and walked to the door of the study. "Would you like some coffee or something else to drink?"

"No, thanks. I'm OK," Guy said.

When Stanley left the room, Guy looked at the paper and remembered another quotation about writing, something attributed to Mark Twain: "Writing is easy. All you do is stare at the blank page until beads of blood appear on your forehead."

Twenty minutes later, Guy still had nothing on the page in front of him, and Stanley came back into the room. He took one look at the blank page and said, "Good thing you're not in the newspaper business, writing under deadline."

"This has always been a little difficult for me," Guy said.

"That's because writing is hard work. But here's a trick that might help: instead of thinking that what you put down has to be perfect, just consider that you have to put something down that may be, in some way, remotely connected to what you want at the end. Write anything that comes to mind. Then write the next thing, then the next. After you fill up a page, take a look at it from the beginning. Cross out the crappy stuff and keep the good stuff, then try to make the good stuff better."

Stanley left the room again, and Guy wrote.

A good leader is someone who is concerned with his people as much as he is concerned with the results his organization achieves.

He looked at the page and thought, "That ain't so bad."

He tries to help his people find work that they're good at and that makes them happy within the organization. He tries to help them learn new things so they can move on to other jobs if they want to. A good leader remembers that people are not machine tools, that they have families and spouses and children and want more out of life than work.

A good leader tries to maintain a cheerful, positive outlook, even when things get bad. A good leader has lots of energy and keeps up with the changes in his business or field. He respects other people and tries to figure out what the right thing to do is, for the customer, the workers, and the organization. A good leader has a plan and sets the direction for the organization, and he gets the opinions of other people in the organization when he is coming up with that plan and the goals that go with it. He lets people know the standards, lets them know what's important to him, and what he expects from them. He is up front about what's important to him, and he is as good as his word.

Stanley came back in the room a half hour later, and Guy showed him the paragraph.

"I'm not a great writer," Guy said. "It's difficult for me. So any suggestions you have, I'm ready to hear them."

"OK," Stanley said. He took a pencil from his desk drawer and made a few marks on the paper, then handed it back to Guy.

"Here you go," he said. "Writing 101. Clear and concise. If you can cut a word without changing the meaning, cut it."

A good leader: is ~~someone who is~~ concerned with ~~his~~ people ~~as much as he is concerned with the~~ and results ~~his organization achieves~~.

~~He tries to~~ helps ~~his~~ people find work they enjoy ~~that they're good at and that makes them happy within the organization.~~ And encourages them to learn new skills ~~He tries to help them learn new things so they can move on to other jobs if they want to. A good leader~~ remembers that people are not machine tools, that they ~~have families and spouses and children and~~ want more out of life than work.

~~A good leader tries to maintain~~ has a cheerful, positive outlook, ~~even~~ especially when things get bad. ~~A good leader~~ has lots of energy and keeps up with the changes in his business or field. ~~He~~ respects ~~other~~ people and ~~tries to figure out what~~ does the right thing ~~to do is~~, for the customer, the workers, and the organization. ~~A good leader has a plan and~~ sets the direction for the organization, and ~~he gets the opinions of~~ involves others in the process. ~~people in the organization when he is coming up with that plan and the goals that go with it. He lets people know the~~ sets standards, lets people ~~them~~ know what's important ~~to him~~, and what he expects ~~from them~~. He is ~~up front about what's important to him, and he is~~ as good as his word.

"Now, use that and rewrite it," Stanley said.
"Yes, sir," Guy said, which made Stanley smile.
"The proper response would be 'Aye, aye.' Try to remember that."
Guy felt good; he could see progress on the sheet in front of him. On a clean piece of paper, he laid out some bullet points, doing further editing as he went:

A good leader:
- Respects people and does the right thing for the customer, the workers and the organization
- Is concerned with people AND results
- Is as good as his word
- Helps people find work they enjoy and encourages learning
- Remembers that people are not machines; they want more out of life than work
- Has a cheerful, positive outlook, especially in difficult situations
- Is energetic and keeps up with changes in the business
- Sets the direction for the organization and involves others in the planning
- Sets standards and lets people know what's important to him and what he expects from them.

Next, Stanley asked Guy to describe a bad leader. Guy went through the same process, without the step-by-step coaching this time.

A bad leader:
- Will lie or stretch the truth
- Puts his own interests first
- Promotes himself ahead of his people
- Is disrespectful
- Won't let me do my job
- Doesn't pull his share of the load.

"Good," Stanley said when he looked over Guy's work. "Here's what I want you to do. You can use this as a guide, although you shouldn't be limited by this, and examine your own leadership style. Which of these characteristics do you have, from either list? How important are they to you? Then I want you to pick the top four values, either stated or implied in what you've written about a good leader, and rewrite them as if you're explaining them to someone else.

"For instance, if you make an honest assessment and find that, yeah, you really do treat people with respect, then you'd put 'respect for others' on your list of values. From those values we'll develop some ethical rules. Those are statements that often start with 'I will.'"

Guy took notes as Stanley spoke, and he left for work the next morning fired up about the next step in this evolution. But instead of spending the morning thinking about values and ethics and how wonderful it would be if everyone treated everyone else with respect, Guy had to listen to Linda Hutchinson rant about the project for John Hulton.

"Before I went to this meeting last week, I didn't think Peter had a clue as to what Hulton wants. Now I know for sure: he's lost. He drew up a plan for this marketing strategy, based on what they told him in their initial meetings. Then John Hulton came to the second meeting and changed everything. He kept talking about 'selling hamburgers,' but I can't tell you what that has to do with his business.

"And we've got another problem: every time Peter talks to those folks, they add more stuff to this sales CD, which doesn't exist yet. And I'm not sure it's possible to get what they want in the amount of time we have left before their sales conference. We're talking about—what?—a little more than a month?"

"So they haven't made a final decision about what they want, and what they do want is beyond our capabilities," Guy said.

"At least you're listening, which is more than I can say for Peter."

"So why am I just hearing about this now?"

"You told me this was Peter's project," Linda said. "He was working with the client, he was keeping you updated, and he was supposed to tell me what he needed from the media side."

"And didn't he do those things?"

"I can tell you only about my talks with him. When he finally did come around, he had a laundry list of things they wanted—interactive features, video, music—that were way beyond the budget. I told him that, but now it sounds like he didn't tell the client, and it sounds like he didn't tell you."

Guy looked down at the calendar on his desk. He had the Concord Sales meeting marked, but he hadn't noted any milestones for the project, as he would have done if he'd been managing it. He'd left that up to Peter. Now it looked like that trust had been misplaced. He felt the constriction in his throat that always came when he was angry, and he knew Linda would hear it in his voice, but he couldn't stop himself.

"So why didn't you come to me sooner? You're supposed to have all this experience ..."

Linda came right back at him.

"First of all, I came to you as soon as I saw what was happening. I'd have come sooner if you'd included me in this sooner. But you put Peter in charge, and he shut me out. Until now. Now I'm here."

Guy didn't have anything to say to that. He didn't like being chewed out by Linda, especially when she was right.

"Secondly, I have about twice the experience that Peter has, yet the two of you treated me like I'm some kind of new hire. I did a project almost exactly like this one about a year before I joined Kensington, and I even saw the exact same screw-ups."

Linda stood facing him squarely. She had quite a head of steam going, but so far Guy really couldn't disagree with anything she said.

"And then there's the whole technology issue. You never sat down with me to ask what kind of capabilities we have, what we can do for the company, what we bring to the table.

"There was that day your neighbor was here, and he suggested that I might have some ideas, and you pretended to be interested."

Guy winced. He had told Linda that he wanted to hear her ideas, and she'd been prepared to meet with him, but he had put her off several times while he put out other fires. They never did have the meeting.

"So you have no real idea what we can accomplish, and young Peter certainly hasn't taken the time to find out. You guys spent all this money to bring us here, and you don't know what to do with us, and you haven't even asked what we think."

Linda was suddenly quiet. Guy looked up from his desk, where he'd been studying the numbers on his speed dialer.

"Are you listening to me now?" she asked. She had a slight smile on her face, but Guy didn't think she was amused.

"Of course," he said. There was more he should add, but all he could think about was wringing Peter's neck.

"I have to find Peter," Guy said. Linda walked away without another comment.

Peter, as it turned out, was working from home.

"Peter," Guy said to his answering machine. "Unless you're physically disabled or have had some horrible accident, I want you here."

By the time Peter showed up an hour later, Guy had learned that the project was in worse shape than even Linda suspected. The client had not even decided on the marketing scheme. Guy began organizing a response, scheduling a telephone conference with the Concord people, inviting Linda and two of her team to sit in. He freed up two other people from the marketing operation: they'd back up Peter, and he'd see to it that the technology people were aware of what was going on right from the opening gambit.

Guy saw Peter's head appear above the top step, and more of him was revealed as he climbed. He looked worried.

"Hulton keeps changing his mind about what he wants," Peter said before he even reached the top step.

"Did you know how far behind you were on this project?" Guy asked. He'd promised himself he wasn't going to lose it, but his voice betrayed his anger.

"I had an idea ... it's not good."

"Why did I have to hear this from Linda?"

"I thought I could get a handle on it," Peter said dejectedly. "This was a big deal for me, being in charge of a project like this, and I didn't want to blow it."

"But if you knew you needed help ..."

Just then the phone rang; it was the Concord team, ready for the conference call.

"Besides, I knew you'd just shoot the messenger," Peter said.

Guy was surprised to hear that, but he was already in a conversation with the client. He pointed at the phone on Peter's desk and mouthed, "Pick up."

In the course of the call Guy learned that Peter's assessment was right: the clients couldn't decide what they wanted. He and Linda made it clear that now was the time; they'd decide today or wind up with nothing. When they ended the call, Linda reminded him that they could still wind up with nothing in time for the big sales conference.

"But at least we have a chance," Guy said. When she looked at him skeptically, he added, "Not a good chance, just a chance."

By 7 p.m. they had an outline, held another conference call and got the go-ahead from Concord. Fortunately for the process, John Hulton was out of the office and couldn't be consulted. At 8 p.m. Guy called Melanie and told her he'd be home late, or not at all. He told Peter to call out for pizza. Placing the order was the most talking Peter had done in three hours.

"He's a little down in the dumps," Linda said when Peter was out of earshot. Guy was surprised to hear what sounded like sympathy in her voice.

"It's his fault we're all here now and will be here 'til God knows what hour," Guy said. "I hope he's feeling it."

Linda gave him one of her meaningful looks.

"Well, perhaps if you'd ever made a mistake, you'd be better able to sympathize."

By 5:30 in the morning they had pulled together a pretty respectable proposal. Guy told everyone to go home and get some rest, but offered to buy breakfast for anyone who wanted to walk to a nearby diner. After an hour, only Guy, Linda and Peter were in the booth. Peter seemed to be waiting for Linda to leave. Finally, he said, "I'm really sorry I screwed up, Guy."

"Happens to all of us, I guess," Guy answered.

Linda told a story about one of the first projects she managed, which involved some lost luggage, a borrowed suit and a presentation she made to the client with her suit pants held in place by a safety pin. They laughed a little too hard and long, all of them tired and strung out on coffee.

"Why didn't you tell me what was happening?" Guy asked.

"Because I know you don't like bad news," Peter said.

Guy was genuinely surprised. "What makes you say that?"

"Remember that woman who used to work here, Debra?"

Guy nodded. No one knew it, but Guy had fired her for lying to him.

"One day she told you about a printing order that was seriously screwed up, and a couple of days later she was gone," Peter said.

"That's because she lied to me about something completely unrelated to that printing order," Guy said.

"Oh," Peter said, surprised.

"And that's a show-stopper, along with stealing."

"Well then, I guess I should have come to you," Peter said. "Sorry."

He slid out of the booth and nodded at Linda, then at Guy.

"I'll be asleep on the conference room floor when you need me to talk to the Concord folks this morning."

"Ten o'clock sharp," Guy said.

"Ten o'clock. I don't know how sharp I'll be."

Then Guy and Linda were alone. During the night she had been a real trouper, offering only encouragement, resisting the temptation to find someone to blame, keeping spirits up.

Somewhere around 4 a.m., Guy asked her how long she had led the media team at Kensington, her old job. Her answer—four years—meant she had twice the team leader experience that Guy had.

The waitress came by and filled their coffee cups again; then Guy looked straight at Linda and said, "OK, what did I do wrong?"

She smiled, and he gave her credit for waiting for him to ask.

"Well, obviously Peter needed to know it was OK to bring you bad news."

"Right."

"And he needed closer supervision."

"But see, I've been talking with Stanley, my neighbor, the guy you met in the office. And he said that you have to give people jobs that will stretch them, or they won't grow."

"Stretch them, not break them. There might be another part to that advice. Maybe you missed class that day."

"What else?"

"You put Peter in between you and the client, in between me and the client, and in between you and me. There was no communication except through him, no way for any of us to get an accurate picture of what was going on.

"And let's not forget that you made me subordinate to Peter by making him the de facto project manager, even though I have more experience in just about everything."

"So you won't work for anyone else? What about me? You have more experience than I do."

"No doubt," Linda said, then allowed herself a smile. "But I think you put Peter in charge because you don't really understand what we—meaning the multimedia and design people—can do for you. And that bothers me, because you didn't make much of an effort to learn."

Guy wanted to lie on the booth's seat and close his eyes. All of Linda's comments were right on the mark, and it was painful to sit through her even-handed critique. At least if she lost her temper he could feel a bit superior, but she was so *right*. He dipped the tips of his fingers in his water glass and pressed them in the corners of his eyes.

"Well, at least Stanley and I will have a lot to talk about," he said.

Guy and Stanley had a lunch scheduled for the day after the all-nighter. Guy postponed the meeting for a week, until the Concord project was almost finished, then called Stanley back to reschedule.

"I'm sorry I had to push our lunch back," Guy said when they met. He'd picked some place a little fancier, a family-owned Italian restaurant that sat at the top of a long flight of stairs and looked over Old City Tavern, where the city's revolutionaries met while plotting their break with England. Guy had proposed to Stanley that Eaton hire him as a consultant, since he was spending so much time training an Eaton exec.

"No thanks," Stanley had said. "A consultant is someone who comes in, looks at your watch, and tells you what time it is. I like to think of myself as a teacher. But you can keep buying me lunch."

"I don't have my homework," Guy said after they'd ordered. "I was supposed to do a self-analysis of my own leadership, but we had a bit of a crisis at work."

"Melanie told us you spent one whole night at the office," Stanley said.

Guy filled him in on the details.

"Bottom line, I just about got burned—badly—for putting Peter in charge of this thing. No disrespect, but your idea about developing people by giving them tasks that are just beyond their reach doesn't look so hot anymore."

"Well, if you were expecting it to be without risk, I guess it does look like a bad idea. But I did tell you that when you let people stretch a bit, they're going to fail sometimes."

"If this had fallen apart, 'failure' would have been an understatement," Guy said.

"So your job as a leader is to set people up so that they succeed and to build a safety net so that when they do fail—and they will at some point—it isn't deadly to the mission or the organization.

"Failure can be a wonderful teaching moment for Peter," Stanley said. "When I fail at something, I'm forced to realize that I don't know everything. And that can make me more likely to listen to other ideas—and to learn.

"Your job, as my leader, is to make sure that you set up the situation so that my failure isn't catastrophic. That's why experienced surgeons oversee procedures when new surgeons are learning. Something goes wrong, the old hand is right there."

"In the past I probably went to one extreme or the other," Guy said. "I was either a micromanager, or I stepped away completely. Now it seems like the answer is in the middle."

"The answer is often in the middle," Stanley said. "When you have someone like Peter, who doesn't have a ton of experience, you're going to stay a little closer. Someone like Linda doesn't need to be watched that closely."

"Speaking of my buddy Linda, I absolutely hate to admit it, but she was great during this whole thing. She jumped right in, started working on the solution instead of complaining about how we got so bollixed up in the first place. She didn't even bite Peter's head off, which I thought was a sure bet."

"So she either likes pulling all-nighters at the office, or she's more of a pro than you've been giving her credit for. Tell me, did your team complain when they had to stay around that night?" Stanley asked.

"They weren't thrilled, but I tried to make light of it, you know? Ordered pizza in, then some beer later on. Of course, I was there with them the whole time, so that might have kept them from complaining too loudly. But I figured I needed to be there, because I was asking them to work so late."

"Well, that's right, of course, but there may be more to it."

"What do you mean?" Guy wanted to know.

"Whose fault was it that the project was so far behind?"

"Peter's," Guy said immediately. A moment later, he corrected himself.

"Ultimately, it was my fault."

"Did you say as much to the team?"

"Not really, no."

"Well, that should be part of your debrief after the smoke clears on this."

"Debrief?"

"A debrief, an after-action review; some people in the military call it a 'hot wash.' You pull everyone together and figure out what happened and why, and most important, how you can make sure it doesn't happen again. This experience is valuable, after all, only if you guys learn from it."

"Doesn't that have the potential to turn into a shooting gallery, where everyone just complains and points fingers?"

"Depends on how you set it up and, most important, how you as the boss react to criticism. You set the ground rules: no personal attacks, keep focused on actions, that kind of thing.

"In other words, I don't get up and say, 'This whole thing was Guy's fault because he's an idiot.' I say, 'This all started with Guy's failure to ... what?" Stanley asked.

"Guy's failure to check the progress," Guy finished.

Their food came, steaming plates of pasta fragrant with olive oil and shellfish. Stanley ordered a glass of wine, then raised it in a toast. Guy lifted his water glass.

"Here's to your willingness to confront all this stuff and try to learn. A leader has to be able to admit he doesn't know everything."

"Thanks," Guy said. "I'm willing to confront my ignorance."

"Puts you way ahead of the pack," Stanley said.

CHAPTER 4

A few days later, Guy took a half hour and closed himself in the conference room with his description of a good leader for a little self-analysis.

"Let's see," he said, looking over the list of attributes, "a good leader ..."

- Respects people and does the right thing for the customer, the workers and the organization
- Is concerned with people AND results
- Is as good as his word.

"OK, Cedrick, you get a minimum pass on those things, I guess." Then he got to ...

- Helps people find work they enjoy and encourages learning.

"Not so much on that one, I'm afraid." Guy put an X next to that line. In part, his difficulties with the Concord account could be traced to his not taking advantage of the talent he had: namely, Linda and the people who came over from the defunct Kensington. He had made a half-hearted effort to match people up with the right work—and that meant looking to challenge them while, in Stanley's words, "sponsoring success." But he didn't take the first critical step: he didn't take the time to learn about his team's capabilities. Worse, he suspected he stayed away from Linda because of the tension between them. The big, tough, former Notre Dame linebacker, who had taken on the NCAA's best running backs *mano a mano*, had been intimidated by a female media graphic designer who had a photo of a cat on her desk.

He laughed at the thought, then allowed himself something closer to the truth: he had been intimidated by Linda's experience. She was his equal, or perhaps even better suited for his job, and he let that bother him to the point of interfering with the work.

He looked a bit further down the list.

- Has a cheerful, positive outlook, especially in difficult situations.

He had done all right during the marathon planning session, but once again, Linda had done a better job. She was the one who kept people's spirits up, encouraging them, joking with them, and never once during the entire night giving in to the temptation to complain about what they were doing. Guy gave himself a *C*.

- Is energetic and keeps up with changes in the business.

"I've got to get out in front on this one," Guy said. The new, larger staff had been together for almost six weeks, and Guy still had no plan for how to integrate them, or for how to put the most effective team together. He'd been spending his time on small distractions, at least in part to avoid thinking about the big picture, but there was more to it than that. Guy had somehow developed the idea that work was all about action, about doing something. Maybe it was all that time on the football field. Playing defense, especially linebacker, meant you were in on, or trying to get in on, every play, every tackle. It was about pursuit, about constant motion. And when he had slowed down, Coach Hadley had been on his case.

Now he was coming to the late realization that business, at least for a leader, might not call for the same frenetic motion. Perhaps he needed time to think. Maybe he should take his team offsite every once in a while for some high-level planning and brainstorming about what was going on.

The last line read:

- Sets standards and lets people know what's important to him and what he expects from them.

Guy put an *F* next to that item.

Stanley had told him to look for patterns, for his own values.

Guy wrote "Respect" at the top of the next page. Then, considering that much of what went wrong happened because he hadn't communicated very well, he put "Communication" on the next line.

He thought about why he'd made Coach Hadley his exemplar for a good leader. He kept coming back to the story about Hadley confronting the team, the alumni and even some of the other coaches after he'd benched the player for pushing his girlfriend. That, more than anything else, was why he admired Hadley.

Guy wrote "Moral Courage" on the page. He knew all about physical courage. Tangling with three-hundred-pound offensive linemen and two-hundred-forty-pound fullbacks had taught him a great deal about fortitude. But when it came to having the guts to do the right thing, the unpleasant thing, the distasteful thing, he wasn't convinced he was in Coach Hadley's league.

Thinking about Hadley made him also think of his exemplar for worst leader: J.W. Eaton. The thing that bothered him most about Wally was that he'd say one thing to your face, then do or say something completely different when it suited him. Guy wrote "Character" on the list of values.

Stanley had told him to explain these values, in writing, as if in a letter. Guy carried the list with him and worked on it in his spare moments over the next week. The night before he was to have lunch with Stanley to discuss them, he showed his list to Melanie.

Respect: A leader treats people with respect, listens to their ideas and is helpful.

Communication: A leader lets people know what he wants. He is clear about the organization's goals, about his personal idiosyncrasies, and in his evaluation of performance, both his own and others'.

Moral Courage: A leader does the right thing, regardless of the consequences, even when it's unpleasant.

Character: A leader acts in a way that will make others proud to be associated with him. Actions are more important than words; words and actions must be consistent.

"What do you think?" Guy asked after Melanie had finished reading.

"I think all this stuff can help us, too."

"That's what Stanley said."

"Remember that little flare-up about the TV? We could have avoided that if we'd both been more clear about what we wanted, I think."

"You want a partner in the financial decisions, right?" Guy said.

"Good," Melanie said, smiling. "Two points for the big guy at the kitchen table."

"And … let me try this while I'm on a roll … you place a higher priority on being able to sleep at night, without worrying about money, than you do on having a huge television."

"Yes, but I also want you to have what you want. You do work hard, and I like to see you get the toys that make you happy."

"But on a more reasonable timetable."

"That's about it," Melanie said.

"What about hot buttons?" Guy asked. "In this description of communication, when I said 'A leader lets people know about his idiosyncrasies,' I was talking about things that get under your skin, that I might not know about, or I might know but choose to ignore."

"Give me an example," Melanie said. "I promise not to get defensive."

"You mean, something you do that bugs me?" Guy said. "OK, when we're out with people and someone makes the predictable jock joke, you know, 'big plus football equals dumb,' you laugh right along with the other folks."

Melanie looked surprised, then contrite.

"I'm sorry," she said, walking behind Guy's chair and putting her hands on his shoulders. "I … you're right. I should be more sensitive."

"Yeah, that's it," Guy said. "Like me. Mr. Sensitive."

"You still want to hear from me, right?" she asked.

"I think I can take it," he said, his eyes closing as she massaged his shoulders.

"Remember the day you told me you bought the TV? And you had Donna on your shoulder in the other room and got her to say 'Fighting Eye-rsshh' with that cute little lisp she has?" Melanie said as she ran her fingers through Guy's hair.

"Sure," Guy said happily.

Melanie grabbed a handful of his hair and pulled down hard.

"*Ouch!*" he said, leaning back to take the pressure off, but he couldn't help laughing.

"That was underhanded."

She slipped her thin arm under his big one. Their relative size—Melanie weighed less than half what Guy weighed—made it a childlike imitation of a half nelson. She tugged at his hair as she made her points.

"You were *using*," TUG, "*your daughter*," TUG, "to look *cute*," TUG, "so that my defenses were down," TUG, "and that, Mister Sensitive Football Player," TUG, "was not fair."

"I give, I give," Guy said. "Uncle, uncle!"

She let go of his hair and walked around in front of him.

"Huh," she snorted, flexing her biceps in a victory pose. "Stanley and I will have you whipped into shape in no time."

At lunch the next day, Stanley looked over Guy's work and pronounced it sound.

"I don't know that I've ever spent this much time thinking about my approach to leadership, or to my relationships, for that matter," Guy said. "Knowing where I'm coming from helps me figure out where I should be headed. It's like having that compass you mentioned a while back."

"Good," Stanley said. "The compass analogy is a good one. You can imagine lots of similarities between a ship without a compass and a floundering manager. This is going to help you get focused. It's also going to help the people who work for you, because you're eventually going to share this with them when you're finished."

"I am?"

"Sure. Remember I said you've got to let other people see this? One of the big benefits of developing a leadership philosophy is that you can let people know where you stand and what's important to you.

"Just think about how much time people spend trying to figure out what the boss wants. Think of the projects that have to be redone, or the priorities reset. Think of the confusion when people can't make sense of one of your decisions. If they have this, they can figure out why you're doing what you're doing. And they can hold you to it."

"Is that always a good idea?" Guy asked.

"Suppose you say, in your philosophy, that you want people to be scrupulously honest, and so they should expect the same from you. You tell them that if you have any doubts, you'll ask for an explanation. And you also tell them to ask you what's going on if something looks fishy to them."

"That's what I'm going to do?"

"Consider the possibilities. In one scenario, every once in a while you have to explain a decision to someone who has a question about your actions. On the other hand, if you've never told them, explicitly, that honesty is important and that it's OK for them to ask you about things, if they do see something that doesn't look right, they're not going to ask for an explanation, and they'll just go around assuming the worst."

"I see your point," Guy said.

"I know that this might be a little scary if you're not used to operating this way. You're going to come right out and say: this is what I believe, and these are the standards. And by sharing them, you're inviting people to hold you to them. That's a higher standard of performance than just assuming everyone knows what you want. The alternative is a boss who doesn't say what the rules are precisely because he wants to change them all the time."

"I can't imagine that leads to a bunch of happy workers."

"Not in tough times," Stanley said. "I mean, I know there are people who achieve certain goals without being honest, or by mistreating people, or by stealing, for that matter. But those kinds of people can lead only when times are good, when the money is flowing and no one is worried about where the next paycheck is coming from. In tough times, or in personal crises, people respond to a leader who has some character.

"If I'm motivated to follow you because you're giving me a 200 percent return on my investment, that loyalty is going to last only as long as those returns last.

"If I follow you because I think you have my best interests in mind and because I'm proud of the association, then I'm not going to jump ship at the first sign that things are going wrong."

Stanley slid a piece of paper across the table to Guy. The heading read "DEPARTMENT OF THE NAVY."

From: Commanding Officer, USS *Nevada* (SSBN 733) (Blue)

To: All Hands

Subj: Command Policy

A. My command policy is developed from my experience and personal philosophy. Your knowledge and observance of these principles will help ensure that USS *Nevada* (Blue) is always ready to perform its mission and that our ship is a safe and reasonable place to work and live.

B.   Ideas and ideals to which I subscribe

1.   Nevada's *mission* is threefold:
   - To keep the peace through the highest state of strategic readiness
   - To maintain the ability to fight and win any conventional encounter
   - To provide each man on board the opportunity for personal and professional success

2.   *Believe in yourself.* Seek and accept responsibility both as a leader and as a follower. Act as if the success of the ship depends on your actions alone.

3.   *Believe in your job.* We don't get paid enough for the hours, the effort, or the dedication it takes to do our jobs, so there has to be something else we value. Take

pride in the fact that your nation depends on you to protect its citizens.

4. *Try to be the best.* You won't always reach your most ambitious goals, but you'll be far ahead of where you'd be if you planned for mediocrity.

5. *A good leader works to make each follower a success.* This sometimes requires both leading and pushing.

6. *The Navy is only as good as its people.* I am personally interested in each of you, your family and your success. Let the command know about your problems. Seek help.

7. *Be a good shipmate.* The sea is a demanding mistress, and we must watch out for each other.

8. *Be proud of your ship.* Show visitors and inspectors how good we are.

9. *Be honest in all you do.* If I can't trust you, I won't keep you on board.

10. *Provide forceful backup to your seniors.* Nobody is infallible. If the ship or someone is headed into danger, take action to bring the danger to light.

11. *Provide steady support to your juniors.* They look to you and your experience to show them the way.

12. *Keep high standards.* If you ignore a situation that needs correcting, you have just established that as your standard.

13. *Punishment should not be the first step in correcting minor errors.* Counseling and instruction are a more constructive approach.

14. *Maintain a healthy skepticism.* "Know" rather than "assume." "Expect" a job to be done right, but "inspect" to make sure it is.

15. *Maintain a "fix it now" attitude.* Take time to plan and perform a job right the first time. If you are asked to do the impossible, register your concern. If told to try anyway, give it your best effort.

16. *Be part of the solution, not part of the problem.* Don't just identify problems; propose solutions.

17. *"Practice daily with the guns."* We must practice daily in order to be able to fight.

18. *Learn to play hurt.* We must be able to continue fighting while combating battle damage.

19. *Training is key.* The crew must know how to operate the ship in day-to-day and emergency conditions.

20. *Give priority to the ship's objectives.* All planning must begin with the overall goals of the ship. It does us no good to have departments reach goals if the ship fails.

21. *Illegal drugs have no place in the Navy.* Alcohol abusers need help as a first step.

C. I will follow these principles with few exceptions. Consider their meaning and apply them to how you do your own job.

S. R. Sabato
Commanding Officer

"You commanded a nuclear sub?" Guy asked.

"Yep. One of the greatest jobs ever."

"This is pretty thorough."

"I'd already been in the Navy nineteen years by the time I wrote that. I had a chance to see lots of skippers—both good and bad—and watch a lot of leaders."

"Were you at all hesitant to publish this? I mean, I can imagine some people using it to sharpshoot every little thing you did."

When Stanley didn't answer, Guy looked up at him. The older man was studying him, the hint of a smile on his face.

"OK," Guy said. "I can imagine some of my people using something like this to take potshots at everything I do. I can imagine Linda Hutchinson waving it in my face and saying, 'Respect? Respect? Where's the freakin' ladies room?'"

"Well, that's always a possibility. But keep in mind that this isn't a written promise that everything you do is going to be perfect. It's a plan.

"If you think about it, the boss who'll be most worried about publishing something like this is the guy who has no intention of following it or who is a shady character to begin with."

"OK," Guy said. "I get it. You're saying I should have the guts to put this out there and be held accountable for it."

"Right."

"Can I start by adapting your version?" Guy asked.

"Mine and anyone else's you can get hold of," Stanley said. "This does not have to be original; it just has to be true to what you believe and want to accomplish."

Guy spent the day working on his laptop in the library of the University of Pennsylvania, which was a couple of miles from his office but not far off his commuting route. His first attempt at a leadership philosophy was wordy, redundant and unwieldy, but by the time he left the library, he had some raw material to work with.

He set it aside for a week, as instructed, and when he came back to it he found it wasn't as bad as he'd feared. He spent some time editing it, then another hour a few days later. When it was pretty tight, he called Margaret, Stanley's wife, asked about Stanley's favorite restaurant, and made reservations there for the following Saturday evening. Melanie insisted that he dress up, and when Stanley came out in a blazer and tie, Guy was glad Melanie had insisted. Guy drove the four of them to Sasso's, and when their wine glasses were filled, Guy proposed a toast.

"Here's to my mentor, Stanley," he said. "You were generous with your time and experience at a time when I needed exactly what you had to offer. I thank you, and I'm pretty sure my team will thank you for what you taught me about being a better leader."

Stanley, uncharacteristically, had nothing to say. Later, Melanie would insist that the old sailor had been a little choked up.

After the toast, Guy pulled an envelope from his pocket and gave it to Stanley.

"This a bribe?" the old man asked. He opened the envelope and read the two-page leadership philosophy.

"This is wonderful," he said, and Guy was very happy.

On Monday morning, Stanley called Guy at work and asked if he'd handed out the two-sheet philosophy.

"Not yet," Guy said. "I was planning to do that today. I'm having lunch brought in."

"That sounds good," Stanley said. "I just wanted to warn you: don't expect too much of a reaction from your people. Chances are good that none of them has ever seen anything like this before, and they certainly won't know all the effort behind it. So hand it out, let them know why you did it, offer to talk about it in private with them—if they want—and settle down to enjoy your lunch."

It went almost exactly as Stanley described it; the team was nonplussed when Guy handed out the sheets. He explained a little about why he did it and how; then there was an awkward silence. Guy couldn't figure out what to say next. Finally, Linda said, "Let's dig in," and the team happily went for the sandwiches.

Guy went through the line last; Linda sat beside him as he ate.

"This is great," she said. She had a beautiful smile; Guy wasn't sure he'd noticed it before.

"Really?" he asked, a bit suspicious.

"Would you coach me on how to do one?"

"Sure," Guy said. "Or you can buy Stanley a couple of lunches and get it from the source."

"That's an idea," she said, tossing a chip into her mouth.

Guy couldn't resist. He asked, "So you really think it's a good idea to do this, huh?"

"I do," she said, looking at him with that intense gaze. "There is one problem, though, and I think you'd better address it right away."

She had become very serious, and Guy braced himself for the criticism.

"You have mayonnaise on your shirt," she said.

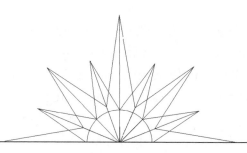

A Leadership Philosophy
by
Guy Cedrick

1. I developed this philosophy to guide my actions as a leader, and I will strive to live and work according to these principles. Let me know when I'm falling short of these goals.

2. My other objective is to clarify my expectations. If something needs elaboration, ask me. I want our team to have an *ongoing conversation* about how we can all become better leaders.

3. My **job** as a leader is to influence people by providing purpose, direction, and motivation, while accomplishing our business goals, improving the organization, living and working according to our values, and supporting people as they try to reach their full potential.

4. My **goal** is to have happy customers and happy employees. Customers are happy when they get excellent products and services for a fair price. We are not in the business of "good enough." Employees are happy when they have some control over their work and their careers, when they are engaged in meaningful work and are treated with respect. I will be concerned with people *and* results.

5. I believe that people want to succeed; my job is to create an environment where that can happen. It's your responsibility to create a vision for yourself and your career. Seek improvement. Be proactive.

6. I will tell the truth, and I expect others to tell the truth. This includes bringing me bad news when it's fresh, when we can still act on it. Bad news can still be good data.

7. You have an obligation to dissent if you disagree with a plan or decision. Have a point of view. Present it forcefully and respectfully, then support the final decision as if it were your own.

8. We must have the moral courage to make the tough calls. If I can't figure out what the right thing is on my own, I'll ask for help. When I do make a decision on a sensitive matter, I'll be willing to explain myself. We

will make ethical decisions if we're open and transparent, and if we're willing to challenge ourselves and each other.

9. I will keep in mind that you have interests and obligations outside of work. To the extent that I can make these aspects of your life fit together well, I will. In return, I expect you to work hard.

10. I will actively seek input and advice. Give me your honest counsel. If I don't think to ask, give it to me anyway.

11. I am committed to honest, useful, two-way feedback. If the way I do that isn't working for you, let me know and we'll adjust. The important thing is that we learn.

12. I will keep my sense of humor, and so should you.

13. I will take responsibility for my actions and decisions, and you must as well.

14. We all make mistakes; they are learning opportunities.

15. When assigning projects, I will balance your need to try new things and learn new skills with the client's needs for the best services we can deliver.

16. Finish your projects on time. If you can't, let someone know just as soon as you figure that out.

17. Communication is the key to smooth operations and to building trust. We will not be afraid of difficult conversations. The after-action review is part of the fabric of our team. We will be honest, and we will not indulge in personal attacks.

18. Take the time to plan and consider contingencies.

19. These things will attract negative attention.
    • If you lie to me or steal from the company or a client, I will fire you.
    • Be on time for meetings.
    • Don't gossip; it is a cancer in an organization.
    • Don't whine.
    • Don't just point out problems; propose solutions.
    • Don't be afraid to say, "I was wrong."

20. I will give you my best effort and I expect you to do the same. When you have ideas, offer them. If there are obstacles you cannot overcome alone, ask for help. I want this to be the best job you've ever had, and I need your help to make it that way.

Chapter 5

Guy Cedrick felt a little bit of panic as he left the meeting with the sales team from Concord Home to walk the half-mile back to his own office. There was a lot to do and very little time to do it all. That much, at least, was a constant in Guy's work life. The pace of operations at Eaton had picked up significantly over the few months since Linda and her team had joined the firm. J.W. Eaton, true to his word, had gone out and found more business. Guy was proud of his team. After a rough start when they were all thrown together, they had figured out a way to work that allowed them to take on the new challenges and thrive.

As he walked, Guy took in the sights of one of the first spring days in Philadelphia. He made his way down Chestnut Street, skirting the park on the south side of Independence Hall, one of the country's most famous landmarks, now framed by the branches of oak and maple trees just starting to turn light green with the warmer weather.

Guy gave a lot of credit to the team, but he also knew that both Stanley and Linda had been instrumental in helping things come together: Stanley because of his ongoing coaching and Linda because she turned out to be energetic and full of great ideas. Guy had figured out quickly that the best thing to do with Linda is point her in a direction and get out of her way.

He wondered if she'd still feel that way after he dropped his giant bundle of notes he had tucked under his arm onto the conference table. The Concord Home people liked working with Guy's people from Eaton and, as often happened, the reward for doing a good job was getting more work to do. While more work was healthy for the bottom line, Guy was only ten minutes into this morning's meeting when he wondered if he was about to be steamrolled by a project that looked much too big for his team and, more to the point perhaps, his own capabilities as a leader.

Guy had texted Linda before leaving Concord and asked her to clear thirty minutes to help him think through something. She was waiting in the conference room when he arrived, laptop in front of her, fingers flying across the keyboard as Guy walked in.

"Thanks for meeting with me," Guy said as he entered, dropping a sheaf of papers on the table. Two sheets printed in color slipped out and shot across the polished surface.

"You seem a little tense," Linda said.

"Yeah, but I'm about to share all this with you so that you can help me worry about it," Guy said, opening the folder with his notes, scratched out on yellow tablet paper. He pushed and pulled the sheets into some kind of order, then briefed Linda on what the client wanted.

"Last year they talked about streamlining the process of applying for a mortgage," Guy said.

"I remember the boss kept referring to 'selling hamburgers,'" Linda offered. "Whatever that means."

"Anyway, now he's thinking that he wants to expand his business. He wants to help clients figure out what kind of home they can afford and how it fits into their overall financial goals."

Guy briefly described the interactive technology tool that would allow a Concord salesperson to enter in information about what kind of property the client wanted, as well as information about the client's finances. The salesperson and client could then take a virtual tour, switching properties in and out of the program while also manipulating the parameters around the loan. There would even be a budgeting tool built in to help people figure out what they could afford. Guy's notes were a series of scribbles, shorthand, and sketches.

"That will be pretty cool once it's built," Linda said. "It also will require some tools we don't have, like the whole budgeting thing."

"Right," Guy said. "Meaning we're going to have to build some partnerships to get this done. But our job right now is to lay out a design. We're not to be limited by what gadgets we already have. We have a big canvas to work on here. We have to tell them what's possible within their budget and time constraints."

"And when do they want all this?"

"They'd like to see some preliminary sketches in three weeks."

Linda laughed. "Why not tomorrow?"

"I know it's tight, especially since we already have a lot on our plate, but I think it's doable," Guy said. "Besides, this whole idea of partnering with technology companies is pretty cool. I think this could be a big development for us in the future. The more types of firms we can partner with, the more opportunities will come our way."

"OK, so how do we organize for this?" Linda asked. "I mean, this is a major push for us. We've got to lay out the work, get teams organized around the various parts...."

"Then we've got to set up some milestones and deadlines, and probably ten other things I'm not thinking of," Guy said. "This is a pretty big project."

Guy paused, looking at the pages on the table. He liked a challenge, and he thought that if he and Linda combined their skill sets, they probably had this covered. But it wouldn't hurt to have another set of eyes, another set of experiences.

"Look," he said. "I've been meeting with Stanley every week or so, kind of a coaching session. Why don't you come with me and we'll see what he can tell us about getting organized for something like this."

"I hope he has some free time on his calendar for the next few weeks," Linda said. "We're going to need the help."

Guy called Stanley after leaving the conference room, then went to brief Linda.

"I think I might have sounded a little panicky when I talked to Stanley," Guy said. "He said we could come over this afternoon."

They left the office within the hour. Guy gave Linda the address but did not see her following him until he pulled into his driveway in the leafy suburb and she pulled in behind him.

"That's a cool-looking car," Guy said when he got out of his own very practical, family-friendly mini-SUV. Linda drove a red two-seat convertible. And although the weather was much too cool to have the top down, it was easy to picture the car that way on a sunny day in the summer.

"It's an indulgence I allowed myself," she admitted. She offered no comment about Guy's car.

"Is Melanie home?" Linda asked. The two women had met at the company holiday party and had hit it off right away.

"I called and she said she'd be home in the next half-hour," Guy said. "We'd like to have you stay for dinner if you can."

"That would be fun."

Guy didn't go into his own house, but walked across the lawn toward Stanley's. Margaret Sabato must have seen them approach; she opened the door before they could ring the bell.

"Hello, everyone," Margaret said. She was a cheerful woman of bird-like proportions, with thick silver hair. Guy bent over so he could plant a kiss on her cheek; Linda, right behind, did the same.

"So nice to see you again, Linda," Margaret said.

"I hope we're not disturbing you," Linda said.

"Not at all," she said before adding, in a low voice, "and Stanley loves your visits."

Guy entered the house and found two teenagers, a girl and a boy, sitting at the dining room table, schoolbooks piled alongside. They stood as Guy and Linda entered. Guy knew that Margaret, who was fluent in French and Spanish, tutored in the afternoon. But he was a bit confused by the math books and scribbled problem sheets.

Margaret introduced the children. The girl, Fahari, and the boy, Ubaro, both shook hands with both Guy and Linda. The girl was shy, but the boy looked Guy in the eye and gave a firm handshake. He gave Linda a dazzling smile and said something in French.

"The children are from East Africa," Margaret explained, "and are trying to learn English at the same time they're learning algebra. So we're spending a little time together to see if we can't get a handle on this stuff."

"Oh, were you a teacher?" Linda asked. "Math or French?"

"Neither," Margaret said. "I was an anthropologist, and for a long time I was what is now called a stay-at-home mom, though I think I just used 'mom.' You know, in my official correspondence." She winked at Guy.

"You'll find Lord Nelson in his study," Margaret said. "Guy, you know your way around. Help yourselves to a beer or soft drink or water."

Drinks in hand, Guy and Linda made their way to the back of the house, where Stanley's study overlooked a small window garden.

"Who's Lord Nelson?" Linda whispered to Guy.

"British naval hero," Guy said. "Margaret's got, like, a hundred names for him. John Paul Jones, Captain Kidd, you name it. She teases him, but they're like two teenagers in love."

"Hello," Stanley said when they appeared in the doorway. "How are my favorite tycoons?"

The three of them sat down around a coffee table, Linda and Guy on a couch, Stanley on a wooden side chair that, Guy knew, had the Naval Academy crest etched on the backrest.

"I've got a little present for each of you," Stanley said. He handed them each a small notebook; each red cover was decorated with what looked like a crown and the legend, "Keep Calm and Carry On."

Guy laughed. "I guess this means I did sound a little panicky on the phone."

"Maybe just a little bit," Stanley said. "But I had this for you before the phone call. Do you know this design? The British government had thousands of posters with this printed on it. They spread them all over the country during the Blitz and World War Two. Such a nice, simple sentiment."

"And exactly what we need to keep in mind as we dive in here," Linda said. "I like it. Thank you, Stanley."

"So what is this big project you just landed?" Stanley asked.

Guy described the client meeting and the list of features the client wanted included in their sales tool. Linda chimed in with a few key points and it was obvious to Guy that she had already given this some thought. Stanley listened. When Guy finished,

Stanley said, "Well, I have no idea how you make such a thing, of course. What can I do for you?"

"Well, this is a pretty big project for us, especially since we have to bring in outside resources. Specifically, a technology company we haven't even identified yet, to build the software that will support this. We'll handle the design—what everything looks like—and we can even do the user-interface."

Linda jumped in. "That's what the user will actually experience."

"Do this and you get this result, right?" Stanley said.

"Exactly," Guy said. "Anyway, we were hoping you could help us break this down into manageable-sized pieces. There must be a way to organize a team around a big project like this. Our team has grown a lot over the last few months, and I haven't faced this kind of challenge before. Frankly, it's a little intimidating."

"I agree," Linda said.

"So you want a way to identify the problem, what it is you want to work on."

"For starters, I guess," Guy said. "Then we've got to look at the resources we have available and figure out how best to deploy them."

"And we've got to assign goals to whatever teams we come up with," Linda added.

"OK, now I'm starting to see where I can help you," Stanley said. "Let's start with your immediate goal. What would you say it is?"

"They want to see some sketches in three weeks," Guy said. "That means a couple of general ideas for the look, but also a few possibilities for the architecture: how the product will act and what it will deliver. We've got to do some homework between now and then and see what's out there, and what's possible."

"I'd like to hear about that meeting that will take place in three weeks," Stanley said. "There are two important questions, at least initially."

Linda took this as a cue, opening her new notebook and pulling out a pen to make notes.

"First is the audience: Who will be there? Second is: What do you want to have happen?"

"Interesting you should bring up the 'who' part," Guy said. "I met the three top sales executives the other day, and they are not all on board with this. The big project is being pushed by John Hulton, who sees a real opportunity here, a chance to do something completely different that will be a huge benefit to homebuyers."

"It sounds great when you say it like that," Linda said.

Guy laughed. "Yeah, but his own sales managers don't agree. At least, not all of them.

"There will be three of them at the meeting in a few weeks. You've got Amy Hoffer, who is in her thirties, I imagine, and whose sales background started with listing agencies. She's comfortable with technology and thinks they should make the effort to use it differently. She's excited about this.

"Then we've got a guy named Sam D'Onofrio. He's got twenty-plus years in the mortgage industry. He's used to thinking of their business in one way, and now he's being asked to think of it in another. But I think he can be convinced.

"The last one," Guy said, scanning his notes, "is Brad Wisner. He seems to be dead set against this idea as well as the bigger program and pretty much anything new. He's got a lot of time invested and has been successful, so he's all about the status quo."

"So what do you want to have happen in this meeting or as a result of this meeting?" Stanley asked.

"I want to convince the sales managers, all three if possible, that these changes are a good idea and that we're the firm to execute the plan."

"But you said you'd just be presenting a preliminary plan, right?" Stanley asked.

"Yes," Linda said. "So we want them to think we're the people to finish the project."

"Good," Stanley said. "Tell me another good outcome."

Guy and Linda looked at their notes. On the mantel, a silver chronograph ticked.

"It would be great if we could get buy-in," Guy said. "Get them participating in the discussion so that they each felt like a part owner, like a stakeholder."

"Great," Stanley said. "So that's different. You're not going to brief them on your ideas. You're going to engage them so that you've all got skin in the game."

"I like that better," Linda said as she wrote furiously in her notebook.

"So one thing you need is a leader's intent for this meeting," Stanley offered.

Guy had not heard the expression before. "What's that?"

"A leader's intent is a clear picture of the desired end-state," Stanley said. "In the military it's called the commander's intent, and it tells you what you need to accomplish even if the whole plan falls apart."

"Which could happen to us," Linda said.

"It can happen to anyone. In fact, it's much more likely that the plan will change—if not completely, then at least in part—before the job is finished. Deadlines change, people leave jobs, requirements and budgets change.

"The Marines have this expression: 'No plan survives first contact with the enemy.' So you've got to know which direction to go in case you have to chuck or amend the plan."

Stanley got up, searched one of his bookshelves, and pulled a title down. He showed the cover to Guy and Linda; it was a history of the Allied invasion of Normandy in 1944.

"So part of the plan for D-Day called for putting about fourteen thousand U.S. paratroopers behind enemy lines during the hours before the landing force hit the beaches. The paratroop commanders developed these elaborate plans, with all kinds of objectives and timelines. Then the planes got blown off course or just dropped people in the wrong places. These guys are lost; they can't find their leaders, their buddies, or their equipment, and many of them don't know exactly where they are. The plan that they had rehearsed for months is out the window in the first hour. What do you do?"

"The leader's intent?" Guy offered. "I mean, the commander's intent?"

"Exactly. Essentially, the commander's intent for the paratroopers was: If everything else falls apart, no matter what happens, we've got to block the German counterattacks against the invasion beaches.

"Now every paratrooper knows what's important, and they can make up plans on the fly that are aimed at that same objective."

"So if we walk into the meeting with one plan and they throw us some sort of curve ball, we still know what we want to have happen," Guy said.

"That's right," Stanley said. "But it's more than that. Think about if you have some member of your team working off on her own, or she's in a client meeting and something changes. She can't get in contact with you because there isn't time or you're not available. She can still make a decision, still make something happen if she's been given a good leader's intent."

Stanley sat down again and took a clean sheet of paper from one of Guy's legal pads. Near the top he wrote "Task," then asked, "What are you trying to do in that meeting?"

"Get buy-in—no, get *participation* from the sales team so that they feel part of the solution," Guy said.

"So coming up with a good enough plan to engage their imaginations is just table stakes in this case," Linda offered.

"We've got to run things so that they feel we're all on the same team."

"Right again," Stanley said. He scribbled some notes, then wrote another heading: "Purpose."

"What is the purpose of this meeting?"

"To get their buy-in. They want us because they're impressed with what we've accomplished and what we've imagined for them. They believe we've got what it takes to get this done."

"Good," Stanley said. "So what does the end-state look like?"

"A meeting where everyone is participating, sharing ideas, and making suggestions," Linda said.

"Is that enough?" Stanley let them sit with the question for a moment before asking, "What does it look like when it's over?"

"They sign off on what we've done and commit to spend money for the next part, which is the actual development."

"That will be much easier to see, to measure," Stanley said. "They'll either put up the money or they won't. Do these three have the authority to spend the money?"

"Yes," Guy said. "They made that very clear to me."

"So that gives us a guide if the original plan falls apart," Guy said. "How do we come up with this original plan?"

"Good question," Stanley said. "Let's talk about goal setting for a bit." He flipped over his notes to a blank page.

"You guys have heard of SMART goals?"

"I have," Linda said. "Though I'm not sure if I remember what each letter stands for."

Stanley wrote the letters "S-M-A-R-T" down the side of the page.

"I do remember the first one is 'specific,'" Linda said.

"Good. Can't have goals that are too big to get your head around."

"World peace," Guy said.

"Noble aspiration; maybe a bit too big for one person to do in a day."

"Measurable!" Linda shouted like she was on a game show.

"You're really getting into this," Guy said.

"Try to keep up," she sniffed.

"Why measurable?" Stanley asked Guy.

"So you know when you've been successful?" Guy said, a bit unsure.

"Of course. The goal line on the football field tells you when you can stop running and start getting ready for the next set of plays.

"Also, you're going to track progress toward these goals, so you can let the team know how they're doing."

Linda had pulled her laptop from an oversized purse and was typing like she was in a speed contest.

"This is great stuff," she said to Stanley without looking up from his notes, which she was copying.

"Next is 'agreed upon,'" Stanley said, writing on the tablet. "You have a better chance of meeting your goals if everyone has bought into them."

"Which means that you've got to engage them early in the process, right?" Guy said.

"My star pupil," Stanley said.

"Yep. Turns out I am trainable."

"Next is 'reasonable,'" Linda said, fingers still flying.

"'Reasonable' works," Stanley said. "I like to use 'realistic,' which implies something different, I think. Maybe more quantifiable."

"You're right. I like 'realistic' better, too," Linda said.

"Last is 'trackable,'" Stanley said, finishing his list. "Sometimes it's tricky trying to figure out how you're going to track progress toward a goal. You've got to identify what you're going to measure so that you know if you're making progress. These things that you measure along the way are called 'Key Performance Indicators.' KPIs."

"What would be an example of that?" Guy asked.

"Well, I can give you one from my world," Stanley said. "Remember I told you how I worked on a program to track repair parts as they moved through the Navy supply system? When we started out, the system just tracked how many parts were sitting in bins, waiting to be used by mechanics. But it turned out that wasn't what was important. The important thing was whether or not increased availability of repair parts reduced downtime for our machines.

"So instead we looked at a maintenance category called 'Not Mission Capable: Parts.' We looked at how many machines weren't working because they were missing a repair part. See? Much more useful information when you're concerned about the repair part system."

"OK," Guy said. "I think I get it. Let me see if I can come up with one from our world."

Linda stopped typing and watched him. She looked like an eager student.

"So part of this project will be creating the content, what the user will actually see."

He drew five small rectangles across the top of a blank page.

"So let's say we come up with five major categories, five areas the user can explore. Each of them will have parts, subheadings, little experiences the user has depending on what he wants to see or accomplish."

Guy drew smaller rectangles in vertical columns under his initial five.

"So in our design let's say we decide there will be a total of fifty of these little experiences to begin with.

"One of our key performance indicators will be how much progress we're making in each category and how much progress we're making overall in getting the designs finished."

"Good," Stanley said. "A couple of other things. Clearly these performance indicators have to be measurable somehow. And everyone knows what the interval is for measuring, that is, how often and when you'll look at progress.

"Another thing to keep in mind is that these various goals and indicators are not just end-states. Leaders use goals to marshal resources and make sure energy is being put to use in the best places."

"What do you mean?" Guy asked.

"Well, if you see one area lagging, it might be time to put some more resources to work there. So the goal isn't something you see at the end, and the team either reaches it or not. A good, useful goal includes milestones so you can track progress towards the ultimate goal."

"This is great stuff," Linda said. "The whole team needs this stuff. Would you be willing to come in and teach a class or two, Stanley?"

"Frankly I think it would be better if you guys taught this as you went along and used it. You'll work hard to master something when you have to teach it to other people.

"There are a couple of other things to think about, too," Stanley said.

"Your team's goals have to support the goals of the larger organization. They've all got to fit together, up and down.

"Someone has to be in charge of the goal. Obviously the leader is overall responsible...."

"Hear, hear," Linda said.

"If I get hanged, you're just next in line at the gallows," Guy said to her.

He turned to Stanley, "You mean someone on each team has to be overall responsible for the goal."

"Yes. And that's probably not surprising given my background. One of the principles of war is 'unity of command.' Someone is in charge, and that person is accountable."

"Someone has to figure out what resources are needed to meet the goal and what the specific action steps are," Linda said. "That would be the leader for that particular goal, right?"

"Yes," Stanley said. "But you don't do that stuff in a vacuum; you include the team, get some help. It's also a good idea to spend some time brainstorming and anticipating obstacles and challenges, and what the solutions might be."

"Cool," Linda said, head down, typing.

"You're going to put all this in a briefing or slides or something?" Guy asked.

"Yes," Linda said. "Since I can't convince Stanley to teach it, I thought it would be useful when you introduce it to the team."

"When you and I introduce it to the team," Guy said.

The next morning Linda and Guy met in the conference room at seven thirty to plan how they were going to engage the team to come up with their goals. She had turned the notes from the meeting with Stanley into slides for a presentation. She showed them to Guy on her laptop. The overview said:

Goal Setting:
Specific
Measurable
Agreed upon

Realistic
Trackable

Another slide elaborated:
- List the benefits from achieving this goal.
- What will you measure to track performance?
- Who is the person in charge?
- What obstacles do you anticipate?
- What steps can you take ahead of time to overcome those obstacles?
- What are the specific action steps to achieve the goal?

"Did you stay up all night working on this?"

"Nah. I got my second wind about nine o'clock and breezed through it. The notes I took, rather, the notes he gave us, were pretty complete and thorough. I added some stuff based on my experience and a few things I found on some websites about management."

"How do you think we should use this?"

"I was thinking that we bring the team in and start with an overview of the project. Then we use this goal-planning stuff to walk through the steps together. That way, everyone has a chance to participate."

"I'd like to come out of this meeting with the teams in place," Guy said. "In fact, I'd like it if you and I could start putting the teams together before we go into the meeting."

Guy stood and listed the names of the team members on the whiteboard. Then he put headings on the board for the teams they thought would begin the work. He wrote:

1. Technology & testing
2. Communication: design user-interface AND ongoing communication with client

The two of them looked at the boards in silence for a moment. Linda pointed at the two big headings—technology and communication—and said, "Which one do you want?"

"Well, I guess it makes most sense for me to find and deal with the outside vendor, since I'm going to have to approve the budget and contracts. That leaves you with the creative stuff and communicating with Concord. You OK with that?"

"Yeah, that won't be the hard part, though," Linda said.

"You talking about Peter and Andy?"

Peter and Andy were Eaton employees who had been on Guy's team before the merger. The two had never gotten along particularly well. Andy was fastidious about everything—his deadlines, his work product, his comportment. Peter cultivated a surfer attitude, even though he had grown up in Pittsburgh and did not see an ocean until he was in his twenties. Peter had become a little more punctual and responsible after Guy shared his leadership philosophy and explained what would and would not cut it. But he back-slid just often enough for people to notice, and since Andy worked with him regularly, it got on Andy's nerves.

"They're both going to wind up on my team, and they both have the experience. They just waste a lot of time and energy butting heads. Maybe it would help if you talked to them ahead of time."

Guy was about to agree, then he said, "I think maybe you should give it a shot first. I mean, if they're going to be on your team, it's important that they see you in a leadership role."

"I'm just not sure I have the patience for their bickering," Linda said. "I'm a pretty patient person, but for some reason those two just get to me. Make me want to knock their heads together or something."

"Well, think of this as a developmental opportunity for you. You're practicing how to deal with problem children."

Linda let out a mild sigh.

"That makes sense, I guess," she said. "I was just looking for the easy way out."

"Aren't we all? If you get in over your head, ask for help. But I think you can deal with it."

Linda stood. "OK," she said. "Let's do this thing."

My team loved the whole SMART goal idea," Guy said when he and Linda met again two days later. "The tech people all have engineering in their blood, I guess. They got very specific on the goals, which made it easier when it came time to break things down into short-term milestones."

He pulled up a spreadsheet on his laptop that showed how his team had broken the technology aspects into segments.

"Everybody left the meeting with a clear picture of what they needed to do and a timeline. And every section has a single person point-of-contact. It was awesome."

"Everybody else left my meeting with a plan of action, too," Linda said. "I left with a headache."

"What do you mean?"

"Andy and Peter didn't waste any time getting into it. Andy just flat-out said that Peter would not make any of his deadlines."

"He said that out loud?" Guy asked.

"I think what he actually said was, 'Yeah, he'll make that schedule when pigs fly.' Kind of under his breath, but loud enough so the people on ether side of him could hear."

"You heard him?"

"Clear as a bell. So did Peter," Linda said. "And I was about to tell Andy to stick around after the meeting, but before I could, Peter shot back with something like, 'At least I've had an original thought in my lifetime.'

"It was surreal. Like being in middle school."

"Holy cow," Guy said. "What happened then?"

"Well, a couple of people jumped in. Beth, who is younger than either of them, got her 'mom voice' on and told them they were not helping the team by behaving that way.

"I thought about adjourning right then, but instead I just asked them both to stick around after the meeting. When we broke, I told them I was disappointed in their behavior, and that we would have a more formal meeting this afternoon.

"I was going to say I had to meet with you, but I didn't want it to sound like I was running to the boss. Like you said, this is part of my development. We'll call it, 'How to Handle Juvenile Employees.'"

"Check this out," Guy said, pulling his laptop closer. "Stanley sent me this link a while back."

"Stanley is on the web?" Linda asked.

"He may not be a 'digital native,' but don't forget he was a nuclear engineer in the Navy. He loves all the newest techno gadgets."

Guy turned his laptop so that Linda could see it.

"When I first read this one on coaching," Guy said, "I thought it was really different from the coaching I had as an athlete. But the more I thought about it, the more I realized that the best coaches—even football coaches—did these things naturally."

Coaching:
- **Purpose/Outcomes:** Clearly define the purpose and outcomes for the session.
- **Flexibility:** Fit the coaching style to the character of each person and to the relationship desired.
- **Respect:** View each person as a unique, complex individual with a distinct set of values, beliefs, and attitudes.

- **Communication:** Establish open two-way communication by using spoken language, nonverbal actions, gestures, and body language. Listen more than you talk.
- **Support:** Encourage people while guiding them through their problems.

"This all makes sense," Linda said. "But I was thinking that our first little get-together with my problem children would be more of a counseling session. You know, 'This behavior won't cut it.'"

Guy thought about it, then said, "You're right. Maybe this conversation starts with your leadership philosophy. Did you share it with everyone?"

"I had a sit-down with every member of the team, most of them one-on-one. I had, as I remember, good conversations with both Andy and Peter. Separately, of course."

"So that might be how you start the meeting," Guy suggested. "Lay out what you won't stand for; then talk about the effect it has on the team when they act this way."

"I wonder if Peter and Andy even recognize the source of their tension," Linda said. "They take different approaches to the same work. Each can be effective, but each of them has to be a little more tolerant of the other's methods."

She looked at the clock on her phone.

"This meeting feels like such a distraction," she said.

"Well, it would be nice if we never had any sort of dysfunction, I guess," Guy said. "But since we're dealing with human beings, that seems unlikely.

"My thinking has changed a bit since I started having all these conversations with Stanley," he went on. "Now I think that this business of helping the team run smoothly so that everyone can deliver a best effort is one of my most important responsibilities.

"When I think back on the people I've worked for—and it's not a long list—the higher up they were in an organization, the less time they spent doing technical stuff and the more time they spent either looking out at the future, at where we needed to go, and just helping people on the team do better. You know, removing obstacles, making connections for people, opening doors.

"I met this one executive from a local bank here in the city, and his little *shtick* was, when he went into a bank, he'd say he was the guy who didn't have a job. 'My job is to help you do your job,' he'd tell the teams. 'What do you need?'

"As a joke it wasn't much, especially after the tenth time, but everybody got it and they asked for stuff they needed."

"I guess that makes sense," Linda said. "If Eaton continues to grow, I can't imagine you'll be doing a bunch of actual design work. You'll get farther and farther away from that."

"I'm not the only one," Guy said.

As Linda walked to her meeting with Andy and Peter, she remembered a story Stanley had told her about something called "Captain's Mast," which sounded to her like a combination of a counseling session and a minor legal proceeding for troublesome sailors. Stanley said that sailors in the nuclear Navy, especially on subs, tended to be an elite group: better educated, older, more mature than most, and therefore the skippers didn't have to deal with very many discipline problems.

Stanley said that his favorite technique was to establish the facts, then outline his responsibility, as commander, to keep good order and discipline and be fair to everyone else in the crew. Then he'd ask the sailors what they thought he should do.

"Inevitably, they suggested much harsher discipline than I thought was warranted," Stanley had told her. "It was like they hadn't thought about the consequences of their actions on the rest of the crew and the ship until that moment. Then, suddenly, they saw what jerks they had been. It was fascinating, really."

Linda found Andy and Peter sitting at opposite sides of the office table near her desk, though they managed not to face each other. The two men were clearly uncomfortable, though Linda didn't know if it was because they didn't like being in each other's company or because they were embarrassed about their behavior that morning.

She handed them each a copy of her leadership philosophy, though they had both seen it before and had even admired it.

Linda Hutchinson's Personal Leadership Philosophy

1. **What I believe about leadership…** As a leader, my job is to inspire and help you achieve your best in service of our goal: a culture that creates awesome products that delight our customers. Here's how we'll get there:

2. **Know when you're the roadie.** Know when you're the rock star. There are times for us to be in the limelight. More often, there are times to set others up to be there. Help your teammates get better; help them succeed.

3. **Have a point of view.** It is your responsibility to understand the context of your work and to help define it. Don't just sit and wait for someone else to tell you what to do.

4. **Wisdom and creativity are all around us.** Being creative is fun and exhilarating and the way to get the best out of everyone. It is our job to access and activate our creativity.

5. **Be empathic and compassionate.** The way to create, inspire, and influence is through the heart—not the head. Listen beyond what someone says and feel why it matters to them—including those above you.

6. **Never stop short of awesome.** Push yourself and the teams you work with beyond what is readily obvious and incremental. Then, raise the bar for everyone through your conviction toward our vision and through stellar craftsmanship—in every detail. Be prepared to fall on your sword for what you believe will get us there.

7. **Get going.** I believe that our best work happens after we get started—not while we're pontificating.

8. **Assume best intent.** No one sets out to fail or create something crappy. Seek to understand one another's approach; help others improve.

9. **You're here because I value you and your superpowers.** Your creativity and skills are what inspire me and how we succeed together. Never let that stagnate.

10. **Create a vision for yourself and your career.** Become aware of what gives you energy and what takes it away. Write it down and declare what you want for yourself in your career. Count on me as your coach to help you create a plan to get you there.

11. **Be open to feedback and learning.** We will all strive to get better. Consider others' ideas. We have an obligation to deliver honest, constructive feedback in a respectful manner.

12. **Our Golden Rules:** Treat everyone with respect. Work hard. Tell the truth. Do the right—not the easy—thing.

13. **I'm a passionate person with a strong vision—but that doesn't mean I have all the answers.** I expect and want your personal creative best in all that we do together. And with that, I hope for this to be the best job we've ever had.

"When I shared this with you just a few weeks ago, did either of you have any doubt that I was letting you know how I wanted the team to run?"

Both men shook their heads.

"Considering how you each acted in this morning's meeting, where would you say you wandered off the straight-and-narrow? Andy, you first."

Andy squirmed a bit before saying, "It's pretty clear that Peter and I don't like each other."

"We'll get to that in a minute," Linda said. "I'm talking about the actions you took this morning."

It looked like it was killing him to speak.

"I was disrespectful," he said finally.

"Can you be more specific?"

"I made a remark about Peter's punctuality."

"You made a lame joke at Peter's expense in a way that was meant to embarrass him," Linda said. "You were..." she turned a copy of the leadership philosophy toward her and pointed at the bullet titled "Our Golden Rules."

"You were disrespectful."

Andy managed to nod his head in agreement.

"Peter?" she asked.

"Yes?"

Peter looked like he was surprised she had addressed him. Linda raised her eyebrows—an unspoken question.

"I took the bait and was just as disrespectful," he said.

"Both of you guys were more intent on getting in your little digs, more intent on indulging your own personal preferences than you were on helping the team," Linda said. "Is that a fair statement?"

When they agreed, Linda went on, thinking of Stanley's story about Captain's Mast. She had a sudden mental image of making Andy and Peter walk the plank. Tied together, maybe. With a big chain.

"So it's my responsibility to make sure the team functions at a high level, so that we produce the best work we can.

"So if you were in my seat, would you look at what you guys did this morning—what you do quite often when you're together, in fact—would you look on that as something that helps the team? Helps me in my job to make us all better?"

"No," they said in unison.

"And do your actions make things easier or harder for the rest of the team?"

"Harder," Peter said.

"How?" Linda wanted to know.

"It makes people uncomfortable," Andy said. "Probably less willing to speak up. Certainly less willing to be in the same room with us."

Linda sat back. Those were good insights and she wanted to let them sit out there for a few minutes. She looked at a copy of her leadership philosophy on the table, then pointed at a line.

"What do you think I meant by this one?" she asked, indicating, "Become aware of what gives you energy and what takes it away."

"I guess it means what we like to do," Peter said.

"And what is that for you, Peter?" she asked.

"I like the creative stuff best. I like making new things from scratch."

"And what don't you like?"

"Feeling hemmed in, not in control of my time."

At the mention of Peter's sense of time, Andy rolled his eyes just a tiny bit. Linda gave him a look.

"How about you, Andy?"

"I like having an idea of what I'm going to do next. I guess I like a good checklist."

"So you two enjoy completely different approaches," she said. "So let's say, for argument's sake, that I want to get the worst possible effort out of Peter. Andy, how would I do that?"

Andy looked at Peter, shrugged his shoulders and said, "I guess you'd give him a deadline and some tight parameters for the work, maybe a whole laundry list of detailed requirements."

"Exactly," Linda said, feeling like she was making some progress.

"And Peter, if I wanted to get the worst possible effort out of Andy, what would I have to do?"

Peter smiled for the first time since he'd been in the room. "Have him work with me."

Andy even allowed himself a small chuckle.

"And why is that?" Linda pressed.

"Because he likes a more controlled environment, I guess," Peter said. "He likes to have some idea about what's next."

"So you guys each want the other to completely change his preference, which is unrealistic and, frankly, unhelpful."

Linda suddenly remembered the story Guy told her about the leader who "didn't have a job," whose sole job was to help others.

"I think one of my most important roles is to create an environment where each person can thrive. I've got to find a way to give you, Peter, some latitude, and at the same time, I've got to provide you, Andy, with the structure that you crave. And all of this has to happen on one team, on one project.

"I think I can do that because I understand that's what needs to happen. But I can't do it unless each of you also understands that other people aren't going to adapt to your ways of doing things.

"Of course, there are some minimum requirements we all have to meet," she said.

Peter leaned forward and rested his forearms on the table. He was finally engaged.

"I've got to adhere to some kind of overall schedule," he said. "Because other people are relying on me to produce work."

Linda turned to Andy, who said, "And I shouldn't try to impose a 'my way or the highway' reign over the rest of the team."

"Perfect," Linda said. "And each of you has to adhere to some basic standards of respectful behavior. No more little tirades like the one we had this morning."

"Yes, ma'am," Peter said.

"Yes, ma'am," Andy added.

Linda laughed, then stood. The meeting was over.

"You know, I kind of dreaded this meeting. Not that I haven't handled, or even been involved in, conflicts like this before. I guess I was just exasperated with you guys, and the bar here was higher."

"What do you mean?" Andy asked, pausing by the door.

"Well, I'm responsible for getting this team to produce some pretty significant results in a short period of time. I wanted the luxury of concentrating on the job, without these distractions.

"But Guy saw this as a developmental opportunity for me. Handling conflict is one of those things I've got to have in my toolbox, I guess."

"Well, I'm certainly glad we could provide you with the opportunity to hone your critical skills," Andy said.

At least, Linda thought, they left the room laughing.

Stanley and Margaret invited Guy, Melanie, and Linda for a barbecue on one of the first warm Fridays of the spring. Eaton had met its first goals and milestones and gotten the go-ahead for the bigger project with Concord Home. Guy was in a mood to celebrate. So was Linda, who showed up with two bottles of expensive wine.

"How is it that you guys got on this track?" Linda asked when the five of them were sitting comfortably around a table set with appetizers. "How is it that Stanley became your coach?"

"I think I made a comment about how his garden tools were so neatly displayed in his garage," Guy said.

"That led to a comment about my service in the Navy," Stanley said.

"And that led to ten thousand non-billable hours of Stanley's patient coaching," Guy said.

"I never said they were non-billable," Stanley said. "They may just be as yet unbilled."

"Well, I appreciate all the help you gave me with my leadership philosophy," Linda said. "That turned out to be really useful."

She told the story of using her leadership philosophy to guide the conversation with Andy and Peter.

"Guy's leadership philosophy also helped us have a minor breakthrough in our communication," Melanie added.

"About the big TV?"

"About the big TV and my unfortunate tendency to go along with 'big, dumb jock' jokes," Melanie said. "Stanley was a bit of a marriage counselor."

"He does it all," Guy said, raising his glass.

"Please," Stanley said, holding up a hand and feigning embarrassment. When no one said anything more, he added, "Please, go on. It's like listening to my own eulogy."

"You know, my biggest observation over the years has been that writing that thing is only the beginning," Margaret said. "It's useless if you don't live it every day."

"Yeah, I thought that 'living the values' meant being all noble," Linda said. "Fighting crime and hanging the occasional embezzler.

"What I found was when Guy said he was going to look after my development, he meant he was willing to throw me into uncomfortable situations.

"I guess it's true you learn only when you're outside your comfort zone."

"I never told you I was hiding outside the door of the conference room that day when you met with Peter and Andy. I was listening in," Guy said.

"You were going to come in and back me up?" Linda asked.

"No I was going to rescue them if you tried to throw them out the window."

"So you guys have hit on a couple of key points, important stuff to think about after you've articulated and shared your leadership philosophy," Stanley said.

The three young people waited to see what came next. Margaret smiled.

"Well," Melanie ventured. "Guy and I had to have a conversation about the stuff he had written. Without that, you really can't get into any depth about how these ideas apply day to day."

"Right," Stanley said. "You've got to start a conversation about leadership and how the team can be better."

"Then you've got to live the values," Linda said.

Stanley held up two fingers. "Right."

"Well," Guy said. "Linda also mentioned development. If you're going to get better, that means you've got to develop your people.

"That is what I was trying to do by asking you to meet with those two guys."

"Good," Stanley said. "So far we've got: begin the conversation, live the values, develop your people."

"What was that other meeting you guys had over here?" Melanie asked.

"Oh," Guy said. "Goal setting. You've got to set goals."

"I would say you've got to meet goals," Linda said. "You've got to get your business results. That's what we're getting paid for."

"Excellent, students," Stanley said. "Very well done. Margaret, what do you think?"

"I think they deserve dinner," Margaret said.

Your Leader's Compass

What is it?

If you've ever spent time wondering what your boss wants, then you know why a leadership philosophy is important. Just as a corporate philosophy or mission statement is designed to let employees know what the organization is about, a personal leadership philosophy is designed to let employees know what the boss is about, what he or she wants, what constitutes good—or bad—performance.

Your leadership philosophy explains the how and why behind your actions as a leader. Writing it will help you clarify your own thinking. Publishing it will let people know where you're coming from. There will be less guesswork, less frustrating thrashing around as employees try to figure out what the rules are, less wasted time, money, and effort as plans are drawn and redrawn in the absence of clear guidance.

Acting according to your published leadership philosophy means you will be a consistent boss. When you are consistent, when people know what to expect, you build credibility. People can trust you.

Inconsistent behavior sends mixed signals, muddies goals, frustrates subordinates, sows distrust and even fear, and wastes the time of everyone involved. If workers cannot predict, with some reliability, how the leader will act, they may be slow to take the initiative. People will adapt to different styles of leadership as long as the leader is consistent. Good leaders act consistently because they know what they believe in, are committed to those values, and act accordingly.

The first step, then, is "Know what you believe in." In the busy work-a-day world, leaders often have difficulty carving out some quiet, uninterrupted time to sit and think about leadership. There are always demands that seem more pressing, fires that need to be put out. Frankly, writing a leadership philosophy is not the easiest exercise; there will almost always be things that are more fun. Yet the failure to think about leadership is analogous to failing to plan. One doesn't need a great deal of experience in business to know that having a plan is better than having no plan.

What's so hard about writing a leadership philosophy? First of all, writing is hard work. It requires patience and persistence, and hardly anyone gets it right the first time. Second, writing a leadership philosophy means the writer has to tangle with difficult, sometimes amorphous questions: What is important to me? Do I value people? What makes me happy? What makes my employees happy? What kind of leader am I? How do people perceive me now?

Finally, publishing a leadership philosophy requires courage. At one point the writer will ask for feedback from people. ("This is how I see myself as a leader. Am I like this, or am I fooling myself?") Finally, the leader will share this philosophy with the whole organization. That means people are going to hold the leader to the promises made and implied in the philosophy. Some leaders will be frightened by the possibility that they'll fall short of their goals, but even the honest effort will produce a better leader.

The goal of all this work is not just a document, not even just an understanding between the leader and subordinates. It is greater self-knowledge, self-confidence, and improved effectiveness as a leader. Your leader's compass

- Provides insight on the leader for both the leader and the followers
- Identifies critical values and beliefs
- Helps establish a healthy organizational climate
- Provides a framework to help ensure the leader's consistency
- Provides a touchstone of values the leader can turn to when lost, confused, or afraid.

What should be in it?

There is no checklist approach for developing a leadership philosophy; each will be unique, because it will be formed by the leader's experiences and beliefs. The best philosophies will explicitly state the following:

Values: What I hold important (e.g., honesty, fairness, respect)

Ethics: Based on my values, what are the important guidelines for behavior

Leadership principles: The behaviors I will engage in and would like to see others engage in (e.g., set the example, take personal responsibility)

Personal idiosyncrasies: My peculiar likes or dislikes (e.g., tardiness, crude humor)

How do I write one?

There are several ways to go about this, but all of them will take you, the writer, on a journey to discover WHO you are, WHAT you believe, what you VALUE, your PRIORITIES, and your EXPECTATIONS of yourself and others.

Here is the technique used by Academy Leadership in its seminars.

1. Start by defining what you think an effective leader looks like.

Take a sheet of paper and divide it down the middle, from top to bottom. Write "BEST" at the top of one column and "WORST" at the top of the other. Think of the best leader you have ever worked for and list that person's characteristics in the appropriate column. What were his or her actions? Values? Skills and abilities, both technical and interpersonal? Do the same on the other side for the "WORST" leader you've encountered. Do not simply write the opposites of what you've written in the first column, but try to define each individually.

An obvious question that comes up at this point is: What does "BEST" mean? The point of this exercise is for you to figure out how you define what you mean by "BEST," based on your experiences.

Compare the columns. Are there similarities in the categories you chose? Does respect—or lack of respect—keep surfacing? Does it look like communication skills are important to your perspective on what makes a good leader? Write a short paragraph describing what makes a good leader and what makes a bad leader.

2. Self-analysis. Using your descriptions and lists, examine your own leadership style and personality. Which characteristics do you have? How important are they to you? To others? Pick the top three or four stated or implicit values and articulate them in writing, as if explaining them to someone else. What ethical rules can be drawn from these values? Write out these rules.

3. Using these values and ethical rules, write the leadership principles you want to model and see in others. These may be in the form of "I will" or "I am" statements; they describe what you to aspire to be.

4. Include your personal likes and dislikes, your "hot button" issues (e.g., "I will fire you for lying.").

This first draft of your personal leadership philosophy should be no more than three pages. Set it aside for a week, then read and revise it. Be clear and concise; if you can cut a word without changing the meaning, cut it. Prefer short, simple words to long words, jargon, or the latest business buzzwords. Repeat this process until you have something that will help your employees understand what you want. The document will never be perfect, so resist the temptation to revise it endlessly.

Publish your leadership philosophy, share it with your employees and associates, and live by it.

ADDENDUM

Some More Thoughts on Leadership
Courtesy of Academy Leadership

Author's Note:

Now that you have read the story of Guy Cedrick and his leadership journey, you may find yourself wanting to know more about leadership. You may find yourself wondering: What *is* leadership, really? Are there certain universal "rules" of leadership? What if my natural leadership style just isn't effective or inspiring? How can I find out where I am, right now, as a leader?

At Academy Leadership, we regularly work with clients who ask these questions and many, many others. In fact, we have created seminars and workshops to help answer them. (Sometimes, looking it up in the dictionary just isn't good enough!) It probably won't surprise you to learn that we have a wealth of materials prepared on the subject. Some materials are from our leadership curriculum. Others are questionnaires or worksheets. All are designed to help people think more clearly about leadership.

I've decided to include some important materials from our curriculum in addition to a self-evaluation questionnaire here. Perhaps they will help you jump-start the process of writing your own leader's compass. If you would like to learn more about Academy Leadership and what we do, please contact us at 866-783-0630 or visit our Web site at www.academyleadership.com. Regardless, I hope you have enjoyed this book—and I hope the following materials will help you clarify your thoughts and beliefs on what it means to be a leader.

Dennis F. Haley

SELF-EVALUATION QUESTIONNAIRE
Prepare2Lead

Assess the status of your leadership philosophy and the extent to which others understand it. What do you really value? What are your priorities? How well have you shared these concepts with the people who report to you? Read the following statements and indicate how often you exhibit the behavior by entering the appropriate number in the box. For example, if you <u>never</u> exhibit the indicated behavior, enter "1"; if you <u>always</u> behave as indicated, enter "4" and so on.

Options
1. Never   2. Infrequently   3. Frequently   4. Always

_____ 1. I often think about the values that are non-negotiable for me.

_____ 2. I have written the definitions of my non-negotiable values.

_____ 3. I live these values and often assess the consistency of my behavior with these values as a check on myself.

_____ 4. I have shared and discussed the meaning of my values and definitions with my direct reports.

_____ 5. My values are consistent with the company's values.

_____ 6. Policies and procedures that I develop and enforce are consistent with my values.

_____ 7. I clearly state my priorities to my direct reports.

_____ 8. I am confident that my direct reports believe that my values drive my behaviors and make me predictable and consistent.

_____ 9. I have stated clearly to my direct reports how I will evaluate their performance.

_____10. I know that my direct reports have a clear understanding about which behaviors I will reward and those that I will not tolerate (and therefore will punish).

_____ 11. I have a well-developed leadership philosophy that I've widely disseminated to my direct reports.

_____ 12. I know that my direct reports fully understand my leadership philosophy because we've discussed it at length.

_____ 13. I have spent time with my direct reports helping them to develop their leadership philosophies.

_____ 14. I consult my direct reports when assessing my consistency with my leadership philosophy.

_____ 15. I take corrective action in changing my behavior when I discover that I have acted inconsistently with my leadership philosophy.

_____ **Total Score**

SELF-EVALUATION QUESTIONNAIRE
Prepare2Lead

ANALYSIS

Determine your total score by adding all of your responses. Check your performance by reading the statements in the box below and then use the WWIDD chart to indicate actions that you will take to improve.

15-29: You probably have not clarified for yourself or for your work team what is important to you. Your direct reports are probably "lost" and cannot look to you for guidance on what to do or how to act regarding leadership behaviors.

30-44: You have obviously thought about what is important to you and act consistently with these ideas most, if not all, of the time. You probably need to spend more time clarifying your core values and leadership principles and share/discuss with your direct reports.

45-60: You have a well-developed leadership philosophy and have shared it, as well as discussed it at length, with your direct reports. Your behaviors are perceived to be consistent with your stated values and they are in line with the company's values. Encourage your direct reports to do the same.

What Will I Do Differently (WWIDD)

Regardless of how successful you've been at developing and communicating your personal leadership philosophy, there is always room for improvement. Identify the items indicating areas needing improvement and determine actions that you can take to improve. Indicate those behaviors in the WWIDD chart below.

ITEM #	ACTIONS TO IMPROVE

"Leadership is not rank, privileges, titles, or money. It is responsibility."
Peter F. Drucker

Why Study Leadership?

Anyone directly responsible for people or for accomplishing goals through the actions of others is a leader by definition. Those who cause others to act by influencing their thinking, decision-making or behaviors are leaders. Leadership is not a function of position; it's a function of role and activity. Organizations require confident leaders who have the *character* and *competence* to lead.

There are at least two major reasons why studying leadership is important. First, the mission of an organizational leader is to achieve the company's goals. Companies either meet goals or fail to achieve them depending upon the effectiveness of their leaders. There is no substitute for effective leadership, nor is there any way to compensate for its absence. The second reason is that leaders must strive to become the best they can be because the people they lead deserve nothing less. An organization entrusts its leaders with its most precious resource: its people. It is the organization's people who do the work, no matter how difficult, no matter how boring, no matter how exhausting. They should expect no less than competent leadership in return. Leaders owe it to those they lead to enable them to contribute meaningfully, to perform to the best of their ability, to know how they are performing, and to develop their full potential.

Leaders are entrusted with a great responsibility. They must embrace the organization's values and learn to apply specific leadership skills. Effective leaders understand and embrace the corporate ideology and have developed their own—their personal leadership philosophy—that is consistent with the organization's. Just as a corporate ideology is the unchanging foundation for an organization's culture and behavior, a personal leadership philosophy is an unchanging foundation for *leader* behavior.

Before developing a leadership philosophy, leadership itself needs to be understood—its definition, its principles and the various styles and their appropriateness under differing circumstances. Likewise, one needs to understand one's self: one's own values, principles, personality characteristics and style tendencies.

Leadership Defined

Because there are many different definitions of leadership, let's begin by articulating the one that we will use here:

*Leadership is **influencing people**—by providing **purpose, direction** and **motivation**—while **operating** to accomplish the goals and **improving** the organization.*

Influencing people. This means getting people to do what you want them to do. There's more to influencing than simply passing along orders. The example you set is just as important as the words you speak. And you set an example—good or bad—with every action you take and every word you utter, on or off the job. You must communicate purpose, direction and motivation through your words and by example.

Providing purpose. Give people a reason to do things. This does not mean that you must explain every decision to the satisfaction of your people. It does mean you must let them know why they are being asked to do something and how they add value to the larger organization.

Providing direction. Communicate the way you want the task accomplished. Prioritize activities, assign responsibility for completing them (delegating when necessary) and make sure people understand the standards. In short, determine how to get the work done right with the available people, time and other resources; then communicate that information: "We'll do these things first. You people work here; you people work there." Know that people want direction, challenging tasks, training and the resources necessary to perform well. Then they want to be left alone to do the job.

Providing motivation. Create conditions that give people the will to achieve, causing them to use initiative when they see something that needs to be done. Give people challenging goals if you want to motivate them. They did not join the organization to be bored. Get to know your people and their capabilities; give them as much responsibility as they can handle, then let them do the work without looking over their shoulders and nagging them. When they succeed, praise them. When they fall short, give them credit for what they have done and coach them on how to do better next time.

Operating. Leaders act to influence others to accomplish short-term goals. Do this through planning and organizing, preparing (laying out the work and making the necessary arrangements), executing (doing the job), assessing (learning how to work smarter next time) and providing feedback on job accomplishment.

Improving. Leaders also focus on the long-term perspective. Although getting the job done is key, leaders must do far more than just accomplish the day's work. Strive to improve everything entrusted to you—people, facilities and equipment. There will be new tasks and goals, of course, but part of finishing the old ones is improving the organization. People respect leaders who assess their own performance, find mistakes and shortcomings, and commit to a better way of doing things in the future.

Leadership Principles

There are fundamental truths about leadership that have stood the test of time. For example, the list below was developed from a 1948 leadership study. They are just as valid today as they were then. Use these principles to assess yourself and develop an action plan to improve your ability to lead:

1. *Know yourself and seek self-improvement.* Understand who you are, including your values, priorities, strengths and weaknesses. Self-improvement is a process of sustaining strengths and overcoming weaknesses, thus increasing competence and the confidence people have in your leadership ability.

2. *Be technically proficient.* Before leaders can lead effectively, they must have mastered the tasks required by the people they lead. When you are a leader, you must train your people to do their own jobs while understudying *yours*, so that they are prepared to replace you if necessary. Likewise, you must understudy *your* leader in the event that you must assume those duties.

3. *Seek responsibility and take responsibility for your actions.* Leading always involves responsibility. Leaders want people who can handle responsibility and help achieve goals. They expect others to take the initiative

within their stated intent. When you see a problem or something that needs to be fixed, do not wait to be told to act. Organizational effectiveness depends upon having leaders at all levels who exercise initiative, are resourceful and take opportunities that will lead to goal accomplishment and business success. When leaders make mistakes, they accept just criticism and take corrective action. They do not avoid responsibility by placing the blame on someone else.

4. *Set the example.* People want and need their leaders to be role models. This is a heavy responsibility, but leaders have no other choice. If leaders expect courage, responsibility, initiative, competence, commitment and integrity from their direct reports, they must demonstrate these qualities. People will imitate a leader's behavior. Leaders set high but attainable standards for performance and are willing to do what they require of their people. Leaders share hardships with their people and know that their personal example affects behavior more than any amount of instruction or any form of discipline.

5.   *Know your people and look out for their welfare.* It is not enough to know the names and birth dates of your people. You need to understand what motivates them and what is important to them. Commit time and effort to listen to and learn about them. Showing genuine concern for your people builds trust and respect for you as a leader. Telling your people you care about them has no meaning unless they see you demonstrating it. They assume that if you fail to care for them daily, you will fail them when the going gets tough.

6.   *Keep your people informed.* People do best when they know why they are doing something. Individuals affect the bottom line results of companies by using initiative in the absence of instructions. Keeping people informed helps them make decisions and execute plans within your intent, encourages initiative, improves teamwork and enhances morale.

7.   *Ensure that the task is understood, supervised, and accomplished.* Your people must understand what you want done, to what standard and by when. They need to know if you want a task accomplished in a specific way or how much leeway is allowed. Supervising lets you know if people understand your instructions; it shows your interest in them and in goal accomplishment. Over-supervision causes resentment

whereas under-supervision causes frustration. When people are learning new tasks, tell them what you want done and show them how to do it. Let them try. Observe their performance. Reward performance that exceeds expectations; correct performance that does not. Determine the cause of the poor performance and take appropriate action. When you hold people accountable for their performance, they realize they are responsible for accomplishing goals as individuals and as teams.

8. *Develop a sense of responsibility among your people.* People feel a sense of pride and responsibility when they successfully accomplish a new task. Delegation indicates trust in people and encourages them to seek responsibility. Develop people by giving them challenges and opportunities that stretch them and more responsibility when they demonstrate they are ready. Their initiative will amaze you.

9. *Train your people as a team.* Teamwork is becoming more and more crucial to achieving goals. Teamwork is possible only when people have trust and respect for their leader and for each other as competent professionals, and when they see the importance of their contributions to the organization. Develop a team spirit among people to motivate them to perform willingly and confidently. Ensure that

individuals know their roles and responsibilities within the team framework. Train and cross-train people until they are confident in the team's abilities.

10. *Make sound and timely decisions.* Leaders must assess situations rapidly and make sound decisions. They need to know when to make decisions themselves, when to consult with people before deciding and when to delegate the decision. Leaders must know the factors to consider when deciding how, when and if to make decisions. Good decisions made at the right time are better than the best decisions made too late. Do not delay or try to avoid a decision when one is necessary. Indecisive leaders create hesitancy, loss of confidence and confusion. Leaders must anticipate and reason under the most trying conditions and must quickly decide what actions to take. Gather essential information before making decisions. Announce decisions in time for people to react.

11. *Employ your work unit in accordance with its capabilities.* Leaders must know their work unit's capabilities and limitations. People gain satisfaction from performing tasks that are reasonable and challenging. They are frustrated if tasks are too easy, unrealistic or unattainable. If the task assigned is one that people have not been trained to do, failure is very likely to result.

Role Expectations

Success of the organization depends upon individuals fulfilling their roles and responsibilities to achieve goals. Everyone, including leaders, has a role—a socially expected pattern of behavior that is usually determined by their status or position in the organization. The degree to which leaders meet the expectations of others and to which others meet the expectations of leaders affects the organization's effectiveness.

Expectations of Leaders. Research indicates that people have common expectations of their leaders. Ask yourself how others would rate you on the following expectations:

- Honest, just and fair treatment
- Consideration of them as mature, professional workers
- The opportunity to work within a climate of trust and confidence
- Acceptance of errors and the opportunity to use them as learning experiences
- Personal interest taken in them as individuals
- Loyalty
- Shielding from harassment from higher-ups
- Anticipating and meeting their needs
- Being told the purpose of tasks
- Clear-cut and positive decisions and instructions that are not constantly changing

- Demands commensurate with their capabilities—not too small and not too great
- Public recognition for their good work.

Leaders' Expectations. Leaders likewise have expectations of others. Assess how clearly you and other company leaders are communicating the following expectations:

- Fulfilling their organizational roles as expected by their seniors
- Being responsible and using initiative
- Demonstrating loyalty by willing and obedient service to instructions, whether in agreement or not
- Having the moral courage to bring conflicts to the leader's attention at the proper place and time and in an appropriate manner
- Using their abilities for the good of the company
- Taking action even though complete information may not be available.

Leadership Styles

People are shaped by what they've seen and learned and by whom they've met. Who you are determines the way you work with other people. Some people are optimistic and smiling all the time; others are pessimistic and sour. Some leaders can wade into a room full of strangers and within five minutes have everyone there thinking, "How have I lived so long without meeting this person?" Other very competent leaders are uncomfortable in social situations. Most of us are somewhere in between. Leaders must always be themselves; anything else comes across as fake and insincere.

Effective leaders adjust their leadership styles and techniques to the experience of their people and the characteristics of their organizations. Treating people fairly doesn't mean treating people as if they were clones of one another. In fact, treating everyone the same way is unfair because different people need different things. Some people respond best to coaxing, suggestions or gentle prodding, whereas others need, and even want at times, the verbal equivalent of a kick in the pants. Effective leaders are flexible enough to adjust their leadership style to the people they lead.

Leaders must take into account individual personality, self-confidence and self-esteem—all the elements of the complex mix of personal characteristics that makes dealing with people so difficult and so rewarding. The easiest distinctions to make are those of seniority and experience. Obviously, experienced people should be led in a different manner from novices. One of the many things that makes the leader's job tough is that to get peak performance, leaders must determine what people need and what they're able to do—even when they don't know themselves.

Leadership style is the subordinates' perception of the leader's behavior pattern when he or she is attempting to influence, guide or direct their activities. Therefore, leadership style is not determined by what the *leader* thinks it is, but by how *others* perceive his or her behaviors. A leader must be constantly aware of this perception and know how to best approach people in each given situation.

When discussing leadership styles, many people focus on the extremes of autocratic and democratic. Autocratic leaders tell people what to do without explanation. Their message is, "I'm the boss; you'll do it because I said so." Democratic leaders use persuasion. There are several shades in between as shown below:

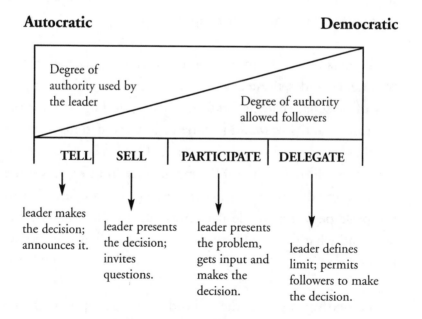

Autocratic   **Democratic**

| TELL | SELL | PARTICIPATE | DELEGATE |

leader makes the decision; announces it.

leader presents the decision; invites questions.

leader presents the problem, gets input and makes the decision.

leader defines limit; permits followers to make the decision.

Competent leaders vary their styles based on the situation, task and people involved. Using different leadership styles in different situations or elements of different styles in the same situation isn't inconsistent. In fact, the opposite is true—using only one leadership style indicates inflexibility and portends difficulty operating in situations where that style doesn't fit.

For the sake of discussion, the continuum is divided into four basic styles. There are varying degrees of the basic styles based on the amount of authority the leader desires to use or delegate. A particular style of leadership might not be successful everywhere and might not be used effectively for everyone. What seems to be a *telling* style to one individual may be interpreted as a *selling* style to another. Sometimes people need to be told what to do because motivation, understanding or experience is low; at other times people need only a task statement to get them going.

Telling. This is characterized by one-way communication where the leader defines followers' roles by telling them what to do, when to do it, how to do it and where to do it. It is natural to expect a leader to use this style when dealing with a novice or during an emergency situation. In fact, people expect their leader to react in a forceful and decisive manner during these situations. It might be inappropriate for a leader to assume this style when dealing with an experienced and competent person, or when the task is complex and the leader lacks sufficient information. Using a telling style in such cases would show a lack of faith in a person's ability, serving only to demotivate him or her.

Selling. Here, the leader uses two-way communication to gain follower support by explaining the reasons behind decisions. This style allows minimal participation by others, but helps them to better understand and buy into the leader's decision. Using this style, leaders explain why they made the decision and then try to sell the decision to the group through persuasion. By taking people into their confidence, leaders gain their support for the decision and motivate them to go along with it.

Participating. The leader allows direct reports to be involved in the actual decision-making process. This requires good two-way communication and the leader's willingness to be influenced by others' knowledge and opinions. The leader discusses possible alternative solutions with the group prior to making the decision. An example of this would be a foreman discussing team members' estimates of completion times for certain parts of a project prior to selecting a course of action for sequencing the job.

Delegating. The leader provides mission-type instructions and minimal supervision. Essentially, the group is allowed to run its own show within the limits provided by the leader. The leader provides people their limits, guidelines, and the necessary authority to complete the task. The leader gives them their mission and allows them to accomplish it as they see fit.

Factors Influencing Leader Style

There are several factors that a leader should consider when deciding upon the style that would be best in a given situation. Some of the factors that affect a leader's style are the individual or group being led, the goal, the situation and the leader himself.

Individual or Group Being Led. Critical areas to consider include individual and group abilities, experience, training, willingness, interest, motivation, group size and composition, and expectations. The greater the ability people have to accomplish the task, the less direct supervision and guidance required from the leader. The greater the willingness to accomplish the task, the less forceful the leader needs to be. Motivation level will determine how much to push and how closely the leader needs to supervise to get the job done. The less the motivation, the more push needed. Leaders need to know what their people expect. This can be important during transition periods between leaders. If the previous leader was a participator and the new leader is a teller, the new leader may observe confusion and have difficulty with communications because of the difference in styles the people are used to and expect.

Goal. The more complex the requirement, the greater the need for specific direction from the leader as to who does what, to whom, when, why and how. If a task requires coordination and attention to detail, leaders do not have much choice in style—they must tell how, who, what and when it will be done.

Situation. The shorter the time available to accomplish a task, the more direct a leader should be. In crisis situations leaders are expected to take charge and make decisions. There is little time for discussions in emergency situations; people look to their leaders for direction and expect concise orders, not questions.

Leader. Leaders' personal values affect their natural tendencies. Leaders' confidence in others and self will also be a key factor. The more confidence leaders have in people, the less they will tend to direct them on how to accomplish a task. The less confident leaders feel about themselves, the more likely they will be directive in nature. Less confident leaders will usually go step-by-step until they feel they know everything is moving along properly.

Personal Leadership Philosophy
Brad Smith
President & CEO
Intuit

Setting Context:
The purpose of sharing this with you is to clearly communicate the ideas and ideals I strive to live up to and inspire in others each day. It represents a psychological contract that empowers you to understand who I am, what I aspire to become, and how you can best work with me and help me and the greater team improve each day.

My Personal Philosophy on Leadership:
- Your title makes you a manager; your people will decide if you are a leader.
- Leadership is not the job of putting greatness into people, but rather the recognition that greatness already exists. The role of a leader is to provide the grand challenge, create the environment, and invest in the individual to inspire that greatness to emerge.
- Leadership is about inspiring a group of individuals to achieve extraordinary things.

The Attributes I Aspire to Role Model Each Day Include:
- **Integrity:** I am a principles-based leader, and will always say what I mean and mean what I say. In the

end, my words and my actions should be synonymous.

- **Humility:** Mankind has many gifts, and I do not view myself as one of them. I seek to learn from others, treat every success and failure as a learning opportunity, and strive to be a better version of myself each and every day.
- **Teamwork:** I believe that a player who makes the team great is far more valuable than simply a great player. A team plays for a cause greater than itself or any individual and believes that only together can we create outcomes that will echo for an eternity.

What I Expect of My Team Members:

- **Be a Learner:** I encourage everyone to aspire to be the best version of themselves each and every day. Be true to who you are and play to your strengths. Equally, be self-aware of your opportunities for personal growth and development. In the end, lean into your learning zone. I prefer the errors of enthusiasm to the indifference of wisdom.
- **Be Committed:** Play to win and seize every opportunity to energize, educate, and empower. Bring a bias for action and set the standard for all else to be measured against.
- **Be Accountable:** We individually and collectively own the outcome. If you ignore a situation that needs correcting, you have just established a new

standard. Don't identify problems without offering a potential solution.

Areas That We Should All Strive to Eliminate in Our Team Environment:

- **Failing to Prepare:** Showing up lacking the context or understanding of the situation, facts, or alternatives diminishes the quality of the outcome, slows the pace of the team, and prevents you from actively contributing—making you the gating factor in the team's success.
- **Failing to Dissent Early:** Harboring a difference of opinion and not offering it up for discussion and debate is passive-aggressive behavior. It minimizes the quality of the outcome and diminishes the effectiveness of execution. If the decision goes another way, be willing to disagree and commit.
- **Failing to Play for a Cause Greater Than Oneself:** A team is only as strong as its weakest contributor. There are no MVPs on a losing team. Therefore, everyone's success is measured by the team's success and should be the highest purpose for which we all strive.

My Commitment:

- To share this with the team members within my organization. Seek their input on how to make it better and seek to live and inspire these ideals daily.

Personal Leadership Philosophy
Dennis C. Parker
President & CEO
Active Minerals International, LLC

My leadership philosophy is based on the principles that I have learned through the study of both strong and weak leaders. It is my belief that following these principles will be the most profitable and rewarding way to lead my life and positively impact the lives of those around me.

I lead by:
- Earning credibility through the achievement of results that exceed established targets for Active Minerals.
- Setting goals that are measurable and achievable. Measurement of progress and taking corrective action ensures success.
- Integrity and character are traits critical to success and the success of AMI.
- Recognizing the success of others is paramount to the success of the company. I express gratitude and thanks for the contribution of others.
- Setting the right example by aligning actions and words with values.
- Making and keeping commitments. Execution of the plan.

I place great value in:

- Honesty. Honesty is not a judgment call or a policy. It is being honest.
- Trust. Trust is earned by delivery on goals and objectives without excuses for failure when it comes. Transparency increases trust.
- Credibility. People who deliver what they promise build credibility and trust with those around them.
- Communication. Clear, concise written and verbal communication avoids error, mistakes, and misunderstanding. Take time to think, take time to write, and communicate in a manner you would like to be treated.
- Accuracy. Elimination of errors and inaccuracy builds confidence in our process, our people, and our customers. Learn from mistakes, accept responsibility, correct mistakes, and prevent mistakes from reoccurring.
- Quality. Exceed the customer's quality expectations to generate customer satisfaction, trust, goodwill, and repeat business.
- Knowledge. Sharing knowledge builds trust, gains credibility, and increases productivity in our company and with our customers.
- Intelligence and Competency. Complex opportunities require people who can fully understand the benefit of win-win solutions and the ability to implement them.

- Listening. Actively listen and focus on what is being said, not what you want to say. Form your reply with care and forethought.

What I expect:
- When you come to me with a problem, bring multiple solutions. Ask questions, get me engaged, and keep me informed. Give me feedback!
- Tell the truth in a timely, accurate manner. Don't delay bad news.
- Work towards your objectives daily. Keep them in focus and plan for success.
- Be proactive in your work and take pride in it. Do your best! Fix it now! Don't wait to be told; don't wait for it to break.
- Protect the company and its interests at all times. Give the company a full day's work for a full day's pay.
- Focus activities on getting results, meeting goals, and helping others do the same by sharing knowledge. Build credibility through results and others will trust you.
- Show respect for the individual in your words and deeds. Learn from those you lead and value their contribution. Invest in their success.
- Be a team player and a team leader.
- Give and accept constructive, fair criticism and make honest efforts to improve. Seek and give feedback to reach your full potential.

- Innovate for the company to evolve and succeed. Understand the risks associated with innovation and communicate them to the best of your ability.
- Know what customers want and what the competition is doing. Deliver what the customer wants better than the competition.
- Do not waste time or words. Make reports concise and to the point. Meetings have an agenda and are results oriented. Make assignments; set times and dates for completion.

Things I do not accept:
- Unsafe working environments, work practices, or willful violations of company safety rules and regulations.
- Lying to cover up a mistake or a misappropriation of company funds. A purposeful omission is the same as a lie.
- Negligence of duty to the company or as a citizen. Do the right thing.
- People who are disruptive, disrespectful, or abusive towards employees, customers, federal/state inspectors, or vendors.
- Individuals who reap personal benefit as a result of their position or control over company resources or activities.
- Any willful act or practice that results in environmental damage that violates state or federal law.

Personal Leadership Statement
Mark A. Turner, President & CEO, WSFS Bank

To Our Team: I provide this personal leadership statement so you can more clearly know what I believe, what to expect from me, what I expect of you, and so you can help me become a better leader.

I am a leader who believes in service, purpose, and strategy. I believe leadership is serving others and working with others to achieve a meaningful mission. I promise to lead by having a positive vision, painting it clearly for others, and providing a sense of purpose in our work. I believe in the power of difference in moving the world forward, so I seek goals and strategies that are clearly different from others' and focus intently on optimizing those.

Because of these beliefs, you can expect me to build things with others—things that are positive, different, valuable, and lasting, and demonstrate alignment of purpose and values in all the things I help lead *(e.g., We Stand for Service and Strengthening our Communities).*

I am a leader who believes in values. I believe solid values create strength, consistency, and sustainability. The values that are most important to me are: character—doing the right thing, even when it is a struggle; genuineness and transparency—letting others see your true self, and a zeal to get to the truth the quickest; fairness—providing both opportunities and rewards based on merit; progress—always moving forward; and grit—getting it done, regardless of obstacles.

Because of these values, I also have "hot buttons." These hot buttons are affectionately known as "Turner's Triggers" and include: bullying, including reckless or unfair statements demeaning others' work product or integrity; obstructive and opaque behavior, including withholding information for personal advantage, and things that are done in secret or with hidden agendas; and sloppiness, including repeated mistakes, thoughtless work, and not meeting deadlines while not communicating that fact in time to adjust.

I am a leader who believes in self-awareness and strengths-based philosophy. I believe self-reflection and constructively acting on it are the best sources of mature growth. For example, I believe I am good at spotting trends, risks, and opportunities in confusing data points and acting on them. I am not as good, however, in spotting risks and opportunities in futuristic things, where the data has yet to be formed.

As a result, you should expect me to help you find what you are good at, and harvest that, and coach you to find resources to augment your shortcomings. You should also expect me to behave the same way for myself.

I am a leader who believes in open communication. I believe in communicating genuinely and with conviction. As a general rule, more communication is better than less, and sooner is better than later. I also believe you can learn the most and improve the most by engaging in candid, meaningful conversations with other people at all levels.

I expect us all to do things out in the open, minimize any human defensiveness we may feel, and respectfully correct for it when we see it in each other and ourselves. When wrong, I expect you to admit it as soon as you suspect it—and when saying sorry would help, to say it. I will lead by example on these.

I promise, at the optimal time and place, to provide you with constructive feedback with the best intentions for the individual, the team, the organization, and our mission in mind. You can expect me to spend time in all areas of the Company and to ask you routinely, "What can I do differently to serve you and be a better leader?"

I am a leader who believes in team, action, learning, winning...and being darned good at what you do. I believe in assembling a group that consists of talented individuals who are cohesive, have extreme clarity of purpose, and are even more powerful as a team. My vision: If I should go into a coma for a year, you will miss me, but not miss a beat. In our daily work, I expect we will set high standards, work hard for the greater good, openly enjoy what we do, and celebrate success. I believe that we are all winners and all want to work on a winning team. I also believe in calculated risk taking…and then managing risks well once they are taken. I know we will make mistakes, and all the things we try will not work, but expect we should take special care to learn from our failures.

Said another way, I believe my primary goal as leader is not, and should not be, to keep the Company, its managers, and its board out of trouble. Leadership includes a willingness to be wrong for others' sake. My goal is, with you, to create long-term value filled with integrity, which will necessarily mean we get into occasional trouble just by the nature of bold risk taking, operating in a dynamic environment, human error, and even mere differences of opinion. I strongly believe that "the perfect is the enemy of the good," and I will take being darned good over perfect every day.

Therefore, even during down times or down moments, you can expect me to continue to invest in the Company's future, your personal development, and maintain a constructive attitude.

I am a leader who believes in well-being and an integrated life. I believe in leading a full, healthy life and integrating career, family, community activities, and personal wellness (physical, mental, psychological, and spiritual) in a way that allows us to prioritize what is most important at that moment.

In doing so, I believe we all will enjoy happier, more productive lives, and the return for the Company will be many-fold.

Because of this belief, and because we have built a strong team to support it, you can expect me to put your personal well-being and family urgencies before the Company's routine business.

Leadership Philosophy
Santos H. Kreimann, Deputy CEO,
County of Los Angeles, CA

My leadership philosophy has been developed over many years of public service to the communities and residents of Los Angeles County. I've been a public servant my entire career, and I view it as a calling rather than simply as a job. I'm grateful for the opportunity to make a difference in the lives of others, and I am humbled to be part of the leadership team of the Los Angeles County Office of the Assessor.

The foundation of my leadership philosophy is built on trust, respect, and integrity. I plan to earn your trust and respect by being of good character, working hard, listening attentively, being decisive, honest and true to my word, and never asking you to do something that I would not do myself. You can earn my trust and respect by being honest and of good character; making sound and timely decisions; owning up to your mistakes; clearly communicating your thoughts and ideas; meeting deadlines and achieving results; and most importantly, putting the interests of your staff and the organization ahead of your own personal ambitions and agenda. The execution of our mission and the growth and development of our staff should always be our primary focus.

I welcome diverse perspectives, differences of opinion, and I do not necessarily view disagreement as a sign of disloyalty.

In fact, I insist on healthy debate during meetings and especially when evaluating alternatives for solving problems. At all costs, refrain from telling me what you think I want to hear. Tell me what I need to know to make sound decisions, and I will do the same for you.

Be part of the solution, not part of the problem. It is not enough to simply identify problems. I expect you to offer your best thinking, to propose innovative ideas and creative solutions, and to identify commonsense approaches to resolving ongoing operational issues. I expect you to participate in evaluating alternative solutions and developing action plans to address strategic or tactical problems we may encounter. Once a decision is made, I fully expect all debate to stop and for all decisions, directives, and/or plans to be carried out by you with professionalism, urgency, and enthusiasm. Anything less is unacceptable.

Take time to plan and perform the job right the first time. If you are asked to do the impossible, register your concern immediately. If directed to proceed anyway, give it your very best effort. I will leave it to you to determine how best to implement any decisions or plans. I will delegate authority and responsibility to the most appropriate staff level and will refrain from interfering and managing the assignment myself. However, I do expect to be kept informed of the project's progress and notified of any delays or challenges in execution, so that together we can make timely course corrections.

I encourage you to exercise initiative and be innovative in

your approach to resolve longstanding problems. Always act without fear of making a mistake, as I understand people will slip up on occasion. I will be tolerant of individual missteps so long as they are not repeated and are not contrary to the goals and values of the office. Always keep moving forward and never quit. Determination and perseverance are two qualities that I deeply admire.

Never walk past a mistake as it serves as a poor example to our peers and subordinates and quietly undermines our pursuit of excellence and our ability to establish a professional, vibrant, and rewarding work environment. If you see something that needs correcting—fix it. If you see unacceptable behavior from a member of your team—stop it. If an employee or customer needs assistance—help them. And, if an employee needs guidance—counsel and mentor them. Be proactive and visible in the management of your staff and freely share relevant information and your expectations with them. I will do the same for you.

Non-Negotiable Items:

- I will not tolerate lying, cheating, stealing, or blaming others for your mistakes. Take ownership of your words, actions, and the results of your decisions.
- Be on time and be prepared for my meetings. Turn off your smartphones or put them on silent, as answering phone calls, texts, and emails will not be

allowed during my meetings.

- Don't interrupt individuals when they are talking. Let them finish their thought before you begin to speak. You will have time to offer your perspective and make your point.
- Be considerate and respectful to your colleagues at all times, regardless of rank.
- I will not stand for individuals who pledge loyalty in public and then spread discontent and gossip in private. I will make every effort to indentify and remove these untrustworthy and disloyal individuals even if they are exceptional managers or high-performing employees.

I've prepared this leadership document to give you some insight on my priorities and on how I intend to make decisions and guide this organization moving forward. It also serves to clarify my expectations of you in meeting our mission of creating an accurate and timely assessment roll while providing exceptional and professional public service with integrity. I am counting on you to hold me accountable in living up to these leadership principles. I will hold you to the highest professional and ethical standards as well. I look forward to working hand in hand with you in transforming this organization into the premiere property assessment agency in the nation.

Now, let's get to work!

Academy Leadership Services: Developing Leaders Your People Want to Follow

In business, good management is about more than technical competency. To be truly successful, managers must also be leaders. That means having the ability to motivate and direct others toward achieving organizational goals. An effective leadership development program not only conveys those important lessons to participants but also shows them how to train their team members to do the same.

At Academy Leadership, we work with your organization to transform managers at all levels into effective leaders who can energize others to accomplish corporate objectives and create tangible business results.

Based on the leadership principles its founders learned at the Naval Academy and West Point—a passion to lead others, a persistence and drive to win, a focus on integrity, and the importance of clarifying each individual's contribution to the overall mission—Academy Leadership training, seminar, and keynote opportunities provide you and your staff with the essential skills you need to achieve business success.

Great leadership skills are at the pinnacle of what drives corporations to succeed. The best way to hardwire these leadership practices at your organization is through extensive and consistent training and leadership development. Read on to learn more about what Academy Leadership has to offer!

Leadership Boot Camp & Performance Coaching

It's no secret that better management results in better organizational performance. But what does better management look like? What is holding your managers back? And how can they become more confident, competent, and successful?

You'll find the answers at Leadership Boot Camp, an intense, specially designed, three-day program that's proven to jump-start manager effectiveness and improve performance. An elite group of instructors—all of whom have forged exemplary careers in the business world after serving in all branches of the world's mightiest military—will train your team. This training combines the top techniques of the world's most successful executives with those of the world's most effective military commanders.

It's a best-of-both-worlds approach for best-of-both-worlds creative thinking, time management, goal setting, communication, motivation, conflict resolution, and employee development. And with 90 days of follow-up performance coaching, emerging leaders will leave boot camp with the support they need to implement the strategies and skills they've learned.

Specifically, your managers will discover:

- The eleven greatest leadership principles ever devised
- Their personal leadership profiles and how to leverage that information
- Four ways to improve communication (and handle data overload)
- Five keys to coaching others in order to improve performance
- Three types of successful meetings, when to use them, and how to prepare for them
- Four steps to conflict resolution and conflict recurrence prevention
- Twelve proven techniques for developing others
- …and much more!

Send your managers to boot camp and you'll get back a group of energized frontline leaders who clearly see the relationship between their daily duties and organizational goals. And thanks to the pointed, personalized leadership philosophies they'll develop, they'll be equipped to instill smart work strategies throughout their teams that both inspire and achieve tangible results.

Leadership Boot Camp & Performance Coaching is like no other leader development program out there. Its military-grounded, battle-tested, business-proven methods will transform managers from any industry, any size company, and with any level of experience into true leaders.

Leadership Excellence & Executive Coaching

In a constantly evolving, uber-competitive, and increasingly connected global economy, what it means to be a leader has changed. The "command and control" model is dead. Not only must you be proficient in your field, you must master a "softer" skill set: creativity, collaboration, the ability to resolve conflict, the ability to motivate, and so forth. So how *can* you get a good grip on the (often-intangible) skills that will help you and your organization thrive in the 21st century?

Academy Leadership's Leadership Excellence & Executive Coaching Course is the game changer you're looking for. It combines military-grounded tactics with cutting-edge business principles. Whether you're a senior executive or an experienced project manager, this concentrated three-day program will give you the tools you need to skyrocket your productivity, performance, and effectiveness.

Under the mentorship of former senior executives and military Service Academy graduates, you will become a more self-aware leader. You'll learn how to communicate your vision, build effective working relationships within your team, and leverage conflict in a way that achieves tangible results. You'll also receive 90 days of personalized post-classroom executive coaching to support you as you implement these highly specific, practical strategies in your organization.

Specifically, you will learn to:

- Articulate your personal leadership philosophy (one of the most critical steps toward dramatically improving leadership)
- Build a higher-performance team
- Align and accomplish organizational goals
- Strengthen your influence with boards, shareholders, partners, customers, colleagues, and critical stakeholders
- Set priorities and develop clear action plans
- Develop committed, energized employees
- ...and much more!

The Leadership Excellence Course is a completely unique approach to executive leadership development. Its concentration on key leadership competencies, along with personalized assessments and coaching, will enable experienced managers in all fields and at all levels to revitalize their careers and drive their organizations forward.

The Advanced Leadership Course

A highly interactive three-day leadership skills training program, the Advanced Leadership Course is a follow-up to the Leadership Excellence & Executive Coaching Course, Leadership Boot Camp & Performance Coaching, and/or the

PMI Five-Star Leadership Seminar for Project Managers. Returning participants will engage with other emerging leaders who have decided to take their leadership skills to a higher level.

This accelerated course will cover advanced topics in modules including:
- Advanced Leadership Communications
- Effective Decision Making
- Leading Change
- Core Values Alignment
- Developing People

Attendees will also have access to a seminar focused on creating one's personal leadership development plan. Moreover, they will have the opportunity to fine tune their personal leadership philosophy (My Leader's Compass) and reevaluate their *Energize2Lead™ Profile* assessment for more effective use with their teammates and coworkers.

The Leader's Compass Course for Senior Executives

An intense four-day executive leadership program led by two of Academy Leadership's premier facilitators, this course is designed for senior leaders at the executive level. Its seminars provide an opportunity to exchange ideas and concepts that will take participants' organizations to the next level of performance.

The Leader's Compass Course for Senior Executives includes the Academy Leadership core programs as well as modules on advanced topics like:

- Advanced Leadership Communications
- Executive Decision Making
- Accountability Compass: Building a Culture of Responsibility
- Coaching Leaders
- Creating a Personal Leadership Development Plan

Senior leaders will complete their personal leadership philosophy (PLP) based on *The Leader's Compass*, a powerful tool that helps them stay on a course bound for success. Executives will discover for themselves that people will follow them if they are truly authentic in articulating their PLPs and will follow up this exercise by communicating that philosophy throughout their organizations.

Lead2Succeed™: Developing Leaders Who Deliver Results

Most managers are technically competent but often lack the ability to motivate and direct others to achieve organizational goals. The Lead2Succeed™ program helps solve this problem by converting managers into leaders who:

- Seek responsibility
- Hold themselves accountable for their own actions
- Train their people as a team
- Make sound and timely decisions
- Communicate effectively
- Plan for success
- Create a positive, enthusiastic, and supportive environment in which their team members can be successful

There are four distinct components:

1. **Strategic Business Performance Assessment**— Quickly pinpoints your organization's capabilities and constraints and evaluates overall alignment and readiness. It identifies the organization's best opportunities for improvement and success.
2. **Energize2Lead™ Profile**—Identifies multi-dimensional characteristics of individual leaders and assesses individual relationships as well as group

dynamics in order to maximize the positive energy needed for effective communication.

3. **Application and Action Sessions**—Are focused on applying the selected leadership skills to accomplishing the organization's most important goals. The training is done in small groups of eight to twelve managers. They attend bi-weekly sessions, which are the heart of the Lead2Succeed™ program. All sessions are multi-sensory, requiring reading, listening, writing, and discussion. After each session participants practice applying the skill in the workplace and report back to the group on what worked and did not work. This sharing of experiences provides a multiplication of the learning experience and creates a common leadership language so leaders at each level can coach and mentor others in the program.

4. **Measuring Results**—Our program is designed to achieve results based on your company's specific goals. Together we will develop measurement criteria and an evaluation plan.

Lead2Succeed™ helps your organization achieve company goals, inspires employees to take initiative in identifying and completing tasks, fosters better communication from the top down to the bottom up, and motivates employees to give their best every day.

The Vision-Based Strategic Planning Process

Where will your organization be in 10, 20, or 30 years—on the Fortune 500 list or out of business? To know if you are succeeding as an organization, you have to know where you are headed. This six-day intensive, interactive workshop helps you and your team create your company's vision and the strategic plan that will help you achieve it.

In addition to the preparation of the vision and strategic plan, we also work with you and your team to develop a systems view of your organization. This enables you to consider options for improving your organizational and management structures and improve your overall business focus and performance. And since changing your corporate culture is often a critical part of the plan, we also incorporate processes for accomplishing that in the workshop, and develop strategies to continue it.

Our proven Vision-Based Planning Process creates for you and your team:

- A vision that is truly shared by all your leadership.
- Clearly defined top-level goals by which to achieve your vision.
- Clearly defined, quantitative objectives by which to achieve the goals.
- Strategies by which to achieve each objective, including strategies for cultural change.
- Action steps by which to accomplish each strategy.

- Implementation plan.
- Metrics—MOEs and MOPs.
- Assigned roles and responsibilities.
- Stakeholder strategies for gaining and keeping their support.
- A War Room report providing the logic trail.

At the end of the planning process, you'll have a vision that is shared by all your leadership, clearly defined top-level goals, strategies for achieving them, a strong, cohesive team, and much more.

Lessons from the Battlefields: Academy Leadership Experiences Explore the Past to Help You Create a Better Future

The Gettysburg Leadership Experience. An excellent opportunity to gain a deeper understanding of leadership, teamwork, and communication, the Gettysburg Leadership Experience brings senior executive teams to the site of the greatest battle ever fought in North America. Through on-the-ground study of the leadership challenges faced by the commanders in this pivotal battle of the American Civil War, participants learn practical, usable lessons that will benefit their organizations today and beyond. Participants gain new insights and new ideas on:

- How leaders can make the right calls amid murky, ill-defined conditions, incomplete information, and high pressure.
- The intricacies of decision making and communication in very large organizations, and how culture affects what's possible.
- How successful leaders share their vision for success, reduce the possibility of misinterpretation, and get everyone pulling in the same direction.
- How leaders develop imagination and courage in themselves and others.
- Why character, a central element of leadership, is the key to building trust on teams.

Our experienced team of leader-facilitators uses stories of key leadership moments to bring critical lessons to life in vivid detail. These lessons, in turn, render valuable insights into how successful leaders operate today.

Modeled on the U.S. Army Staff Ride, a technique used to train officers in leadership and decision making, the experience lets participants see and feel, as no history book or mere lecture can, the challenges commanders faced during these three pivotal days in our nation's history. Instructors provide the historical background and facilitate in-depth discussion to reach a deep understanding of "leadership in action." Executives leave excited about their opportunities to be better leaders and armed with battle-tested tools they can use immediately.

The Normandy Leadership Experience. Learn how to lead at the site of one of the world's great military operations—the 1944 Allied liberation of France. During the four-day program, you'll see and feel the challenges that were faced by commanders in WWII's pivotal battle. Instructors illustrate "leadership in action" by facilitating in-depth discussion on topics such as the strong character of Dwight Eisenhower and how it kept the allies working together, how exceptional leadership led to the victory of Pegasus Bridge, and how leaders kept their soldiers moving forward in the face of adversity on Omaha Beach. During this one-of-a-kind learning opportunity, you'll gain new insights and new ideas on how to:

- Build flexible organizations that carry on in the midst of chaos and rapid change.
- Develop leaders who are creative thinkers.
- Communicate strategic intent so that everyone understands and takes responsibility for the mission.
- Earn the trust of subordinates.
- Build strong coalitions, across cultures and generations, for competition in the global marketplace.
- Prepare the next generation of leaders.

Best of all, you'll leave the experience armed with battle-tested tools you can use immediately.

The American Revolution Leadership Experience: Concord Bridge. In the Concord Leadership Experience, executives visit the Minute Man National Historic site near Concord, Massachusetts, flashpoint of the American Revolution, to learn timeless lessons on leadership that can invigorate today's businesses. During a visit to the site of this 1775 day-long battle, participants learn practical, usable lessons about team building, morale and courage, dealing with ambiguity, effective communication, and the execution of strategic intent. These powerful tools will help leaders to energize their organizations and get them moving towards their business goals.

As with our other on-the-ground leadership experiences, walking this historic ground creates a learning atmosphere that is almost impossible to create in a conference room, because the experience, like leadership, is emotional as well as intellectual. Executives gain new insights and new ideas on:

- How leaders help the organization combat fear and uncertainty.
- The intricacies of contingency planning and war-gaming.
- How an organization's culture can be predictive of performance.
- How leaders influence morale.
- How leaders organize effective teams.

Participants leave ready to meet the challenges of leading in today's complicated business world head on.

Out of the Trenches: Inspirational Leadership Messages to Help Improve Your Organization

Are you looking for that perfect speaker or perfect subject for an annual company dinner, a professional association, or part of a larger event? The Academy Leadership staff has experience in speaking on a variety of leadership topics, such as leadership philosophy, productivity improvement, how to motivate people, how to manage conflict, how to develop future leaders, and more.

We can tailor a presentation to your audience and your specific needs. Whether you choose a keynote speech or one of our workshops, our programs will allow you to apply leadership principles to your organization's current situation. Your next company dinner could be the perfect opportunity to share valuable lessons in leadership with your staff.

Lead the Way Today!

If you would like to take part in one of Academy Leadership's results-driven workshops or training programs, or if you would like to book one of our speakers for your next company event, visit www.academyleadership.com or call us at 610-783-0630.

Books from Academy Leadership Publishing

The Leader's Compass: A Personal Leadership Philosophy Is Your Foundation for Success, 3rd Edition
(2013, ISBN: 978-0-9727323-8-3, $27.95)
by Ed Ruggero and Dennis F. Haley

The Leader's Compass for Law Enforcement Professionals: A Values-Based Approach to Influencing People, Accomplishing Goals, and Improving Your Organization
(2012, ISBN: 978-0-9727323-7-6, $24.95)
by Roy E. Alston, PhD, and Dennis F. Haley

The Accountability Compass: Moving from "The Blame Game" to Collaboration
(2012, ISBN: 978-0-9727323-9-0, $24.95)
by Dennis F. Haley

The Core Values Compass: Moving from Cynicism to a Core Values Culture
(2010, ISBN: 978-0-9727323-5-2, $24.95)
by Dennis F. Haley

The Corporate Compass: Providing Focus and Alignment to Stay the Course, 2nd Edition
(2009, ISBN: 978-0-9727323-6-9, $24.95)
by Ed Ruggero and Dennis F. Haley

My Father's Compass: Leadership Lessons for an Immigrant Son
(2006, ISBN: 978-0-9727323-4-5, $17.95)
by Perry J. Martini

Inspiring Leadership: Character and Ethics Matter
(2004, ISBN: 978-0-9727323-2-1, $24.95)
by R. Stewart Fisher and Perry J. Martini

Academy Leadership books are available at special quantity discounts to use as premiums and sales promotions, or for use in corporate training programs. For more information, please call Academy Leadership at 610-783-0630, visit www.academyleadership.com, or write to: 10120 Valley Forge Circle, King of Prussia, PA 19406.